# Natalia Makarova

## BALLERINA

By the same author

# NATALIA MAKAROVA
## *Ballerina*

RICHARD AUSTIN

DANCE HORIZONS
1801 E. 26th St., Brooklyn, N.Y. 11229

*First published in 1978*
*by Dance Books Ltd*
*9 Cecil Court London WC2N 4EZ*
*Printed in Great Britain by*
*W & J Mackay Limited Chatham*

.

American edition first published in 1978
by arrangement with Dance Books Ltd., London

ISBN 0 87127 103 6

Library of Congress Catalog card number 77–94038

# Contents

# Illustrations

# ILLUSTRATIONS

*For the dancers of the Kirov Ballet*

Feed apace, then, greedy eyes
  On the wonder you behold;
Take it sudden as it flies,
  Though you take it not to hold.
  When your eyes have done their part,
    Thought must lengthen it in the heart.

SAMUEL DANIEL
*From* Tethys' Festival (1610)

# *Acknowledgements*

MY GRATITUDE TO Miss Natalia Makarova is, I hope, best expressed in the following pages, since but for her patience, encouragement and consideration, this book could never have been written. I should also like to thank Madame Galina von Meck who, despite the demands of her own literary work, kindly translated a number of items for me from the Russian. I am grateful to Miss Dina Makarova who provided me with much useful information relating to the period from 1970 to 1975, and to Miss Diana Davis of S. A. Gorlinsky Ltd., who gave me details of Miss Makarova's performances abroad in 1976 and 1977. Once again I must thank Miss Mary Scudamore who helped me correct the typescript and the proofs.

For permission to use copyright material, acknowledgements are made as follows: for a quotation from 'Crazy Jane Grown Old Looks at the Dancers' from *The Collected Poems of W. B. Yeats*, to M. B. Yeats, Miss Anne Yeats, and the Macmillan Co. of London and Basingstoke; for a passage from 'Deer on the High Hills' by Iain Crichton Smith, published in his *Selected Poems*, to Victor Gollancz Ltd.; for a quotation from *Tonio Kröger* by Thomas Mann, translated by H. T. Lowe-Porter, to Secker & Warburg Ltd.; a quotation from Maxim Gorky's *My Childhood*, translated by Ronald Wilks and published in Penguin Classics, is reprinted by permission of Penguin Books Ltd.; to Mr. Richard McKane for his translation of a poem by Boris Pasternak in *Post-War Russian Poetry*, edited by Daniel Weissbort, published by Penguin Books Ltd.

# *Introduction*

THIS BOOK is not a formal biography, although it contains a considerable amount of biographical detail. It tells the most mysterious story of all—the making of an artist—and seeks to trace the sources of her art, lost though these are in the ambiguities of the past and in the hidden world of her own creative imagination. When we confront genius we move in a strange land, and there is for us no certain way, no final destination. I have tried, as far as I have been able, to let Natalia Makarova describe her art in her own words, and I have created much of this book from her own ideas, based on discussions with her over the years. This study, therefore, deals exclusively with her artistic career, and does not concern itself with her private life, except in so far as this relates to her dancing in such matters as her memories of childhood—the source of an artist's vision—and her experience as a ballerina in the Soviet Union.

In later years a time will come for a full and detailed biography; it is too early yet for any final word, for she is now entering the greatest creative period of her career, and I can only guess how far she is going to lead us, into what new worlds of the imagination. I have glimpsed within her dancing a wider truth than any I have ever found in theatrical art, but, in a sense, it is still unknown to me, though I have tried to describe it times without number now. In this dancing we can obtain hints, moments of sudden insight; yet even as we seem to grasp them they elude us, and we are left, baffled, to ask our questions to the empty air. What remains after these astounding performances is, I hope, contained in this book; what is within them can be discovered only when she dances on the stage, and her art flowers for us again, mysteriously and each time anew.

The purpose of criticism is, in my view, to celebrate great art; as Gautier says, it tells of the adventures of the soul in a world of masterpieces. If one is to celebrate, one must praise, and from a full heart; one has only to read Hazlitt, Gautier or Levinson to see how unashamedly they praised the artists they most admired. We live in an age when we are small-minded about genius: we pick away at masterpieces, instead of trying to recreate them in our imagination; and this was not the way the greatest critics wrote.

In this book I have sought to give a series of impressions of the ballerina, attempted with all the powers of evocation at my disposal to recreate in parallel images the elusive texture of her dancing, the tonal colour she conveys in different roles. It is not objective: one can be objective about plumbing or algebra, but not about great art. Indeed in a sense this is no more than the story of how one critic, enamoured by her genius at his first glimpse of it, sought it out like a rare species over sixteen years, and tried to capture it in a net of words. It is her story; and it is also, in part, my own.

*Country of Wonder* and *Romeo and Juliet*
(Kirov Ballet)

*Romeo and Juliet*
with
Anatoly Nisnevich

Anton Dolin's
*Pas de Quatre*
(Kirov Ballet)

# ONE

# *The Child*

IN LONDON, on the fourth of September, 1970, Natalia Makarova, *prima ballerina* of the Kirov Ballet, Leningrad, sought political asylum in the West. It was the penultimate day of the Kirov Ballet season at the Festival Hall. This step, she realised, was irrevocable, but there was no other way in which, as an artist driven by a profound inner need and sense of dedication, she could fulfil her destiny, her search for truth in art.

The search, she knows as all artists know, is finally unavailing; the resolution is never achieved, even though it may be glimpsed momentarily in all its distant harmonies, its sublime proportions. Such a quest has been beautifully described by her fellow-countryman, Boris Pasternak, who, driven by the same impassioned longing for the truth within himself, writes:

> In everything I want to get
> to the real essence.
> In work, in search for the way,
> in the heart's turmoil.

> To the essence of past days,
> to their causes,
> to the basis, to the roots,
> to the core.

17

# THE CHILD

All the time catching the thread
of fates, of events,
to live, think, feel, love,
to make discoveries.

I would lay out my poems like a garden.
With all the tremor of veins
in single file and in lines
lime trees would flower in them in succession.

I would bring into poems a breath of roses,
a breath of mint,
meadows, sedge, haymowing,
the rolls of the thunder.

The play and trials
of triumph achieved—
the drawn bowspring
of a taut bow.

This is the story of the planting of that garden, and now its full
flowering in the high summer of her art.


The mysterious springs of a great artist's creative life are not easy to
find, though one can take the acceptable way and pretend to discover
them as though they leaped in broad daylight. Truth can be forced
into an artificial design if one is prepared to impose a pattern on it,
set in order the chaos of all the lost years. But, looking back, there is
no path through the dark wood; only a few tracks that straggle away
into nothingness, or fall out of sight, or even draw us, at first hope-
fully, but then to no known destination.

When she was a child on holiday Natalia Makarova loved to run
away from her parents into the forest. They were afraid and could not
find her, but she knew the way; she never got lost, however far she

ventured out of the sound of their calling. Yet to her now that childhood is a dark mystery, deeper than any forest. In some ways she feels she has never really found her path out of it, still amazed at the child she was, in the same manner as that child wondered at her own nature in the secrecy of her heart. Perhaps with all artists there is this sense of disquiet over what they once were, and what they now seek to become; indeed in that lost childhood is hidden the source of all great art—the intensity of experience, the vivid colours, the glare of light and the ominous darkness, the dazzle of high noon. She has felt nothing since, Makarova told me, so intensely as then—no misery as total, no joy so swift in passing, or then so far beyond recall.

I wish it had been easier: that at an early age she had developed a passion for dancing and music, or been swept away in wonder by the art of Galina Ulanova, or even that, like her illustrious predecessor, Anna Pavlova, she had wanted as a child to be the Princess Aurora in *The Sleeping Beauty*, when no other aim would conform with her dreams. But it was not so; the making of this career has been for her a kind of accident, a series of improvisations; indeed she will say, 'I have no career: it has not started yet'. She becomes impatient when I try to fix her to some moment of insight or illumination when she discovered her future. It is not, she says, as easy as that; you cannot manipulate the truth so, not even for your artistic designs. And she cares for emotional truth passionately; it is the source of her art, its single guiding star that she trusts above all others.

However, perhaps one might choose one incident from the past to give us a moment's insight, when we can observe how, all unknowing, a small child first confronts her destiny. When her mother had gone out and she was alone, Makarova would go to the mirror, stand facing it and weep. They were real tears she wondered at and the sorrow was real; yet she watched, still and absorbed, confronting her grief. And one part of her, she tells me, rejoiced in it: here was the tragic heroine, a miniature Odette with her immortal tears. Her misery was complete; she was alone, lonely and frightened, yet it was beautiful to her also, a grief mysteriously apart, set in its solitude like a single rose. It is a picture that throws a long shadow into the future, to the great tragic roles she was destined to play—Giselle, Odette, Manon and Juliet, whose truth she has been able to discover in her own heart. At that moment before the mirror, Makarova told me, she truly grieved; it was not play-acting, a game of make believe, and yet she was able to observe herself with such clarity, such calm detachment, even as she measured the extent of her own unhappiness.

Here, I think, lies the duality of the true artist. He is both a spectator and a participant—the one who suffers, and the one who also observes his suffering. At the worst he becomes completely narcissistic (and Makarova agrees that all ballerinas are to a large extent narcissistic and self-absorbed in their own emotional life), eternally fascinated by his image as he multiplies it in his fantasies, in all the adventures of his imagination.

This curious duality is wonderfully captured by Jerome Robbins in his ballet, *Afternoon of a Faun*, where the couple, a man and a girl in a ballet studio, are for a long time oblivious of one another, fascinated only by their reflections in the classroom mirror, in the same manner as Natalia Makarova once watched herself, a lonely, puzzled child. She admires the ballet enormously and wants to dance in it herself. I think it is the symbolism that appeals to her; it answers a need to search deeply within her own nature for a truth that can be expressed only in movement, and the attitude, at once detached and committed, that contains it. Dancers are absorbed, almost obsessionally so, in their own bodies; it gives them this odd remoteness from life, so that there is a sense of isolation around them, an inner concern that we cannot ever penetrate.

Yet the greatest of dancers transcend the essential narcissism of their art, for they have a remarkable empathy with others to whom they speak in the dance in a communication at the deepest level of personality. Their dances become allegories of the human spirit, a statement in truth and total sincerity. Such dancers are rare creatures: few indeed in the long history of the dance, and one of them is Natalia Makarova, *ballerina assoluta*, and maybe still, in part, that child who wept at her image in a glass.

Natalia Makarova was born in Leningrad on 21st November, 1940. Like Anna Pavlova, whose early life bears striking resemblance to her own, she was an only child, brought up through the first years by her grandmother to whom she still remains devoted. Her father and mother came from different worlds, her mother's parents being of country stock, while her father, an engineer by profession, had lived in a far more sophisticated and cultured milieu. Her grandfather was an architect with three sisters, whom Makarova remembers, were women of considerable intellectual distinction, one of whom, a brilliant linguist, attempted to teach languages to the young Natalia when she was at school.

Six months after her birth the war broke out, and for two years Makarova's life was fragmented as a result. Communication between families became difficult, sometimes impossible to maintain, so that when her father lost touch with his family they were never afterwards to be certain of his fate, whether he was killed at the front, or lost perhaps among all the sad armies of refugees that moved across the country. Her mother moved from place to place, seeking a secure home for herself and the child, as the war brought with it chaos and disruption. Finally she decided it would be best for Natalia if she were to remain with her grandmother in the country where she could find a measure of peace and security. The next three years were spent in a little village far from Leningrad, during which time Natalia was completely separated from her mother.

Makarova's grandmother was, at heart, a peasant woman. The

strains and conflicts of post-revolutionary Russia had passed her by, and she remained within a traditional way of life that had not changed since the time of the Czars. Deeply religious, serene, attached to country ways and in tune with the rhythms of the changing seasons, she is still almost totally in ignorance of the vast Soviet tyranny that has grown around her. Absorbed in her own quiet life, the passing of the Saints' days and the sublime rituals of the Orthodox Church, she lives in a changeless world, wider in its horizons and more richly composed of prayer and repose than anything the Soviet bureaucrats could fabricate for their new society. When Makarova speaks of her it is with a kind of protective tenderness that is full of memories of the past, even to the sounds and scents of the country around her in those early days. Her grandmother, Makarova says, has had an influence on her character and art very similar to that of Pushkin's beloved nurse, Rodionovna, to whom he wrote so many of his poems.

As Makarova remembers it, the war does not seem to have touched her or affected the life of the village. She was completely caught up in the slow and traditional pattern—in the farms, the animals, the round of seasonal activities. Her grandmother used to take her to the village church each week, though she was later, when she began to grow up, to lose interest in religious matters as she became absorbed in the atheistic world of communist dogma where the church is for the old, irrelevant to the young and the society in which she lived. Now she has returned to a view of life that contains a sense of a spiritual reality beyond herself, though she would not call it religious in any doctrinal sense. Maybe, however, the seeds of belief sown by her grandmother did not die in the dark earth of a materialist philosophy, but ripened at last in these later years.

Listening to her speak of those early memories, I was reminded of a passage from *My Childhood* by Maxim Gorky, when he writes of his own grandmother in these terms:

22

When she spoke she seemed almost to sing her words and this made them take root firmly in my memory, like flowers—soft, bright and full of richness. Before she came into my life I must have been lying asleep in a dark corner, but now she had woken me up, brought me out into the light, and bound up everything around me into a continuous thread which she wove into many-coloured lace. At once she became a friend for life, nearest to my heart, and the person I treasured and understood more than anyone else. It was her unselfish love of the world that enriched me and nourished me with the strength I would need for the hard life that lay ahead.

Even today, when she faces a difficult performance or a new role, Natalia Makarova will telephone her mother and ask that her grandmother should pray for her. Those qualities of Makarova's inner life that I should describe as religious must have their roots deep in that early childhood. They have given her a reverence for life, for music and painting, indeed a kind of wonder with which she confronts the world and a curious simplicity in her trust in God, that is one of the most touching aspects of her personality. I am not alone among her friends who are asked to pray for her before a performance that worries her; sufficient that she feels we are in accessible reach of God!

At the age of five, the war over, she was brought back to Leningrad, a weakened and impoverished city, still bearing the terrible scars of the siege, still heroic in the memories of its suffering. Her mother had remarried, her stepfather being a jazz musician. Three years later her stepbrother was born—a beautiful child to whom Natalia at once unfavourably compared herself. They settled down in a big flat on Tchaikovsky Street which was occupied by several families. There they were to live continuously until she married at the age of twenty. Natalia and her parents occupied one room. Life was hard, food rationed only a little above subsistence level—clothes, shops, any of the usual amenities of a city being non-existent. Her mother made all her clothes, while her stepfather grew skilful in stitching and repairing her shoes. They were very poor in a city where poverty was a commonplace. One can have little concept of the hardships in Leningrad after the war—the people moving around the rubble, the boarded-up shops, the lack of transport, entertainment and any sort of social life.

She recalls how it was a serious matter when she lost her ration card, so that even the little it provided was not available to her family for a week until the authorities issued her with a replacement. They were not hungry, but they ate very simply, and it was a major event in the family when some small luxury was acquired to break the monotony of their diet.

Natalia worked very hard. She would get up early, sometimes at about six o'clock, to do her school work before class. She was an exceptionally clever child, and was able to read and write far earlier than most children. When her class-mates were still struggling with the elements, she was deeply immersed in the world of Jules Verne, and she can recall how, in boring classes, she used to lift the desk lid a fraction and read *Twenty Thousand Leagues under the Sea* through the crack provided.

This is, for Makarova, the strangest period of her life, since she can give no real explanation to herself for the hostility she felt towards her mother and her stepfather. She is now totally devoted to her mother, whom she telephones frequently, and it is the greatest sorrow of her present life that they are parted from one another, and, by the cruelties of political ideology, must remain so.

It is not the right of a biographer to psycho-analyse his subject, and I do not intend to probe into the subconscious of this lonely, puzzled child. But one can see how her disrupted infancy, the long separation from her mother, even, perhaps, the over-protective attitude of her grandmother, must have led to this state of inner hostility. To find her mother remarried to a man who was a complete stranger to her, and to know, for the first time, the rivalry of a small stepbrother who had, she remembers, this angelic face and

24

curly hair, so different from her own straight, flaxen hair, and those dreamy, slightly muzzy features that stare out at one from old photographs—all these things were bound to cause a turmoil in the mind of a child of five.

At once she felt isolated, perhaps even unloved. She thought she was ugly. When her mother, drying her after a bath, once remarked on what a long back she had, she considered herself entirely disproportioned, far inferior in looks to her pretty stepbrother. Her mother and stepfather were puzzled, even, she says, a little afraid of her, so unpredictable were her moods, so excluding her long silences. She would come home from school, not say a word of greeting, and sit down at a table and begin her work. They did not know how to approach her, and, realising this, she gained a sense of power over them, a curious private triumph, even at the moment when it was darkened by the melancholy that surrounded it.

There is no doubt that Natalia's mother was too strict, too anxious to make her daughter a model of rectitude and good behaviour. She was frequently punished, and brought up in so disciplined a manner that it is not surprising she should have rebelled. This is, indeed, a characteristic that has marked her whole life up to the present time, and may, in part, be a reason for her extreme individuality and the fierce assertion of her own independence which she values so much. It is a contrast that also marks her artistic life, in that she is obliged to conform to the disciplines of the classical style and the academic technique, while, at the same time, working always to find her own freedom of expression within them.

It was not as if she did not love her mother, nor feel a kind of protective concern for her small stepbrother; indeed, when once on holiday in the country her mother tried to punish him, she came to his defence, then to run away on her own into the woods. She stayed out all night, only coming closer to the house to listen if they were still calling for her, then, satisfied, to retreat again out of hearing. She was also not without imagination when contemplating some act of retribution, even on one occasion placing a live hedgehog in her mother's bed. It smelt, she remembered, quite badly.

Makarova recalls a curious incident from this time, small in itself, but made interesting by the vehemence of her reactions. One day at lunch her mother was cutting up a melon, and the young Natalia was making endless difficulties about what slice she required. At last, exasperated, her mother tried to knock her hand aside with the knife, and succeeded only in cutting very deep into the tops of Natalia's fingers. (She has the scars to this day.) Blood poured out, and her mother became almost hysterical with terror. But Natalia, despite the pain, was exhilarated, her delight so intense she had seldom known such happiness. Here was drama and she the heroine; here was retribution on her mother from the blind gods who would plague her henceforth with guilt; here was the intensity of experience for which the child yearned. For Natalia it was marvellous, in a sense the first role she had ever played.

Her greatest delights as a child were the summer holidays in the country. Yet here again her attitude to nature is not a commonplace one. It is not and never has been enough for her to look at a beautiful view, to be an observer, however acute; she must experience it in the world of sensation. She needed to lie on the grass, to put her hand into the running river, to touch the surface of the leaves. She will often describe her sensations in relation to natural things in her elegant but fractured English as being 'biological', by which I take her to mean that these must be experienced in physical terms. In her life there is a concern for emotional truth as there is for intellectual honesty, but her apprehension of the world and her delight in it is basically a very child-like one, despite the subtlety of her intellect and the clarity of her thought. This attitude is typified for me in a remark she made about her defection from the Kirov Ballet, with which I shall deal later, when I asked her what she did when she was in hiding in a country house. Her face lit up. 'Oh, it was marvellous,' she said. 'I picked mushrooms.'

Each year Natalia used to go on holiday with her parents to Latvia. She can still recall her stepfather balancing a vast suitcase on his head, her mother laden with parcels and her small stepbrother running on ahead towards the train, and the huge excitement of the long journey. The family rented a small isolated cottage, lost among the huge landscape of woods and undulating hills. She loved the solitude, to run by herself through the woods, to collect blueberries and mushrooms, or dream away the long summer afternoons in this great silence, the distant landscape spread around her.

In conversation Makarova is inclined to stress the unhappy aspects of her childhood, perhaps because these memories darken her imagination, and bring back pictures of her beloved country that she is unlikely to see again. One misses in her recollections the sense of gaiety and high spirits that are so much a part of her nature, even if, at times, these are quenched by moments of sadness that seem to her to come out of nothing, swoop down suddenly like some terrible bird of the night. But the wayward, moody child, creature of impulse, of abrupt kindnesses, open, generous, sometimes indiscreet, is still with her, still observant behind her beautiful, seeking eyes. (I recall her ironical comment on some minor indiscretion, that she envied the man in the Russian proverb who could 'jump into the river and come out dry'.) She is, in some ways, quite unselfconscious, again like a child. When she was preparing for her first performance in Kenneth MacMillan's ballet *Elite Syncopations* to Scott Joplin's music, she would startle her friends by suddenly dancing phrases of it in the street, watching her reflection in shop windows. It did not seem to her an unusual thing to do. Certainly she cut short my protests by stating firmly that mad people were not noticed in Kensington!

The sensation of the power latent within her body appears to have come quite early, as she adored to do acrobatics, and sometimes would pounce on her mother—at the most difficult and carefully chosen moment when she was carrying a pair of saucepans in her hands—and leap on her back in the first rudimentary *pas de deux*. Like so many girls she loved to dress up in old clothes and pose in front of the mirror in some tragic role. Typically, she always saw herself in terms of tragedy.

As she grew older, she began to read all the Russian classics, the plays of Shakespeare, and also Galsworthy's *Forsyte Saga* which kept her completely enthralled. She accepted, quite naturally, all the dogmas of a communist society with which children were indoctrinated from an early age, and it was not until much later, when she was in her early twenties, that she first began to question the philosophy and ideals of a communist state.

At the age of twelve, Natalia joined the ballet club at the Pioneer Palace in Leningrad. The Pioneers is the youth organisation of the Communist party, and all children—unless they have a reputation for very bad behaviour—are obliged to join it. At that point she had no intention whatsoever to make the ballet her career; to attend ballet classes was no more than a hobby, and she used to go there in her free time three evenings a week. Because of her long legs and neck, her companions nicknamed her 'the giraffe'.

She chose the ballet classes in a somewhat arbitrary manner, due to the enthusiasm of some of her friends, but it might just as well have been some other subject—painting, literature or gymnastics—in which she was particularly interested. It seemed to her a nice way of relaxing after school, and it would also bring her new friends, since she was by temperament lonely and in need of companionship. Indeed it is true to say that she discovered her vocation in life almost by accident, and she often thinks that it might well have been some other. Today there is no artist in the ballet more dedicated than herself, yet it is a kind of dedication that grew on her, due to her insistent inner demands for some form of high achievement, rather than one that in any way she felt as a child. One can say that she became a dancer by accident, even as she became a great dancer by design.

Her first stage appearance was something of a disaster, since, in the role of a snowflake (which, it seems, is an obligatory part for all children in ballet both in the East and the West) she got extremely muddled, and, what is worse, caused chaos among the other dancers who found her panic-stricken improvisations a serious risk to the cohesion of the whole *corps de ballet*. There is a delightful scene in Jerome Robbins' ballet *The Concert* that portrays such an incident exactly. Makarova puts this disaster down to her absent-mindedness, from which it seems unlikely that she will now ever be fully cured.

She enjoyed the classes, although she was sometimes in trouble for arriving late for them—another constant trait, very Russian in character, that makes her complain even now that it is more or less impossible to arrive in time for class, however well intentioned she may be. Sometimes I feel she wears a wristwatch more for decoration than utility.

Makarova discovered early the price all artists have to pay for their gift. And it is a high one. Measured in terms of suffering, perhaps too high. As a child and later as a young dancer, she felt different from others. She said that they seemed to recognise it, and, however friendly she became, however closely she approached them, they seemed to draw away from her. She always felt alone, isolated; in the company of others she felt the loneliest of all. They did not seem to accept me, she says, there was always this distance between us. How exact a description it is of that cruel bargain life makes with the talented. Thomas Mann, writing of literature in his superb story *Tonio Kröger*, describes this with wonderful precision:

> Literature is not a calling, it is a curse, believe me! When does one begin to feel this curse? Early, horribly early. At a time when one ought by rights still to be living in peace and harmony with God and the world. It begins by your feeling yourself set apart,

in a curious sense of opposition to the nice regular people: there is a gulf of ironic sensibility, of knowledge, scepticism, disagreement between you and the others; it grows deeper and deeper, you realise that you are alone . . . .

It is a long way from the opera houses of Europe and America to that strange child observing her grief in a mirror, but the child and the great ballerina would, I think, recognise one another, perhaps even with a shared compassion.

On an impulse, without consulting anyone or letting her parents know of her intention, Natalia Makarova, at the age of thirteen, presented herself at the door of the Vaganova School of Ballet in Leningrad, to begin her studies as a classical dancer. It was the first of several impulsive actions that have shaped her career, the one that she says has hardly yet begun. She does not know for certain what took her to the Vaganova School, for even then she had no great ambitions to be a professional dancer. It was just an impulse, she tells you, leaving your questions to hang, baffled, on the air.

# TWO

# *The Dancer*

THE VAGANOVA SCHOOL is attached to the Kirov Theatre, formerly the Maryinsky, home of the Russian Imperial Ballet. From the Maryinsky have emerged those immortal figures of the dance, Pavlova, Nijinsky and Karsavina, whose influence was the major inspiration in the establishment of ballet as a distinctive art form in the West. Russian ballet is now more than two centuries old, having been founded in 1738, and the great traditions of the classical dance have been maintained unbroken at the Kirov despite all change and revolution to the present day, where its dancers remain unrivalled as its most complete exponents in our time. Natalia Makarova is thus the guardian of a great inheritance of which she is rightly proud, and she comes to the ballet of the West as its most noble example whose dancing may well have a profound influence on the future of ballet in both Europe and the United States.

Today the Vaganova School is the largest of its kind, not only in the Soviet Union, but also in Europe. It trains an average of five hundred students from all parts of the Soviet Union and from many foreign countries, particularly those of the Eastern bloc. It accepts children from the age of nine who have completed their elementary school education. The period of study is normally nine years before students are eligible to join the Company at the Kirov, though, in Makarova's case, as she arrived later at the school than is normal, this period was reduced to an intensive course of six years.

Like so many schools that have been modelled upon it, the Vaganova School provides an academic as well as a dance education. It covers the same syllabus as that taught in Soviet secondary schools, including literature, history, mathematics, physics and the French language. On the dance side it includes character dances as well as the classical ballet; also mime, the history of the theatre and the ballet, music and the history of art. At the end of the academic year graduation concerts are held, and a few members of the school then join the *corps de ballet* of the Kirov.

Makarova's decision to join the Vaganova School, made with all the implacable will of her obdurate thirteen years, met with fierce opposition from her family; indeed, she tells me, it became a family scandal. But nothing would budge her, and if it seemed to them a precarious and wasteful career, even if (as they doubted) she had any talent for it, so her determination to prove them wrong led to her rapid progress through the school. Life was arduous, the day beginning with lessons in classical ballet lasting at least two hours, followed by academic school work. After a scrappy lunch, there would be further classes in character dancing and mime. Although they were taught the history of ballet, no mention whatever was made of contemporary ballet in the West, which was, therefore, for the students, non-existent. They would appear at the Kirov in performances of such ballets as *The Sleeping Beauty* where children would be required.

It was a difficult life for a young girl who had been brought up in a sheltered environment in her earliest years. A high standard of academic success was demanded, and the ballet classes were long and arduous, more so than in Western schools, and made even more testing for Natalia as she was obliged to cram a nine year period of study into six years. Her gifts must have been recognised very early, though she could not realise this, feeling only that she was often driven to a state of near exhaustion for no purpose at all. Her mother used to give her fifty kopeks a day to buy her lunch in the school canteen, where, she tells me, the food was quite appalling. Often she

*Swan Lake* with
Sergei Vikulov and
*Corsaire pas de deux*
with Yuri Soloviev
(Kirov Ballet)

The mad scene from
*Giselle*

Rehearsing the second
act of the ballet with
Yuri Soloviev

missed lunch, so that she could go to the cinema or buy ice-cream instead. She always loved the cinema, and has retained this interest up to the present time.

Like all imaginative children she day-dreamed, but not of being a famous ballerina, since she remained curiously detached from her work at the Vaganova School, but of making her mark in the world, of being someone extraordinary who lived a life of high but ill-defined romance. One is, however, still confronted by the fact (so inconvenient for a biographer) that she did not see herself as *prima ballerina* of the Kirov, or even begin to imagine the future that awaited her. She had been taken in a school party to performances at the Kirov, where they sat high in the top gallery, but she remembers little about them, and cannot now recall either the work or the dancers. She does, however, remember that the Kirov Theatre provided excellent ice-cream. But there was no vision of glory there, nor were her ambitions fired to emulate one day the ballerina on that historic stage.

The directors of the Kirov found her at times stubborn and rebellious; the more conventional of these considered her too modernistic in her approach to the role, while she would not readily accept a traditional manner of playing in classic parts. It is a paradox that all artists must be constricted in the form in which they work to achieve the greatest freedom of expression, and this paradox is central to Makarova's life both as a person and a ballerina. She could not, either as a child or as a woman, have striven with such determination to be free both in choice and in artistic purpose if she had not, from early on, been aware of the narrow boundaries set around her freedom.

The political indoctrination in Marxist theory continued, but on the whole the students were not interested; if they discussed politics at all it would be to mock at the pomposity of some official or government decision, this being a long tradition in Russian life as we can discover from the plays and novels of Gogol and other writers of his period. Even a modern writer who usually conformed to the Party line, Ilya Ehrenburg, could laugh at the pomposities of officialdom, and be rewarded at times with a bleak smile. Makarova grew interested in modern Russian literature, particularly in the poetry of Mayakovsky and the novels of Bulgakov. She accepted the Soviet view of life and world affairs without question; she even wept when Stalin died. The gradual disillusionment was to come later.

It is from the Vaganova School of Ballet that nearly all the dancers of the Kirov Company are recruited, so that they share a common style that is so distinctly their own; in expressiveness, freedom of movement and elegance, they are the true aristocrats of the classical dance, far in advance of any ballet company in the world. In them the academic technique has been extended to its furthest limits, without at the same time in any way losing its proportions or the purity of line that are the inheritance from the Imperial Theatre. But now it is richer in emotion, wider in scope and warmer in humanity than any other technical method evolved in the formal dance. The School has produced a series of great ballerinas, including Marina Semonova, Galina Ulanova and Natalia Makarova, while in the Company today there are a number of young soloists from whom the greatest dancers of the future will emerge. Much can be said in criticism about ballet in the Soviet Union today—the poverty of its choreography, the dead hand of officialdom that lies across every form of experiment, its absurd insularity—yet it has been true to its inheritance and the great traditions of the classical dance.

Agrippina Vaganova, who died in 1951, her life's work complete and miraculously displayed in the dancers of the Kirov Ballet, was directly linked with the teachers and dancers of the old Imperial Theatre. Together with Anna Pavlova she was a pupil of Yekaterina Vazem, who was Marius Petipa's favourite ballerina. She studied under Nicolai Legat, and frequently attended as an observer the classes of Enrico Cecchetti, so that she came from an impeccable lineage, fostered by the two masters who have contributed most to the development of the classical dance both in Russia and the West. Coming under the influence of Michel Fokine, she began to incorporate his own ideas of a freer expression in movement into her teaching methods, and from this synthesis of the old and the new the Vaganova system evolved over the years.

Vaganova sought to give the dance a far greater plasticity, particularly in the carriage of the arms and back. Kirov dancers are recognised by their superb *épaulement*, the sweep and freedom of their movements, particularly of the arms, long extensions in *arabesque* and their exceptional high and floating jumps. She spoke of her method as 'dancing out of the body', where the muscles of the torso originate the movements that then grow out of the body almost organically, in a manner quite different from dancers educated in other schools. I do not deny that there is a danger in the Vaganova method that the classical line will be lost in attempts to achieve the greatest plasticity in movement, where the dance would then be debased into the exaggerations of the Bolshoi school; certainly among the present ballerinas of the Kirov, Alla Osipenko, for example, is a superb dancer, but her classical technique has become flawed by too great a concentration on *plastique*. Yet this need not be the case: both Makarova and her former colleague, Irina Kolpakova (who was Vaganova's last pupil) are remarkable for their extreme purity of style and concern for the classical line.

It is interesting that the Russian ballet critics, even from Makarova's earliest days at the Kirov, found her originality and individuality as a dancer not at all easy to understand. Yet they were quick to recognise the singularity of her vision. They write of a 'search towards harmony' both in the music and the character, the modernity of her approach to familiar roles, the sense of an inner quest which one critic describes as 'a striving for truth'. In one revealing passage we learn how choreographers were nervous about creating roles for her because of her individuality and refusal to take a traditional line in her dancing, preferring to experiment, and to search (as one critic describes it, 'restlessly') for a personal vision. Indeed she is rebuked for being 'unruly and stubborn', as she is also criticised for excessive modernism and a reliance upon intuition, rather than on a detailed, carefully studied version of a role. One sees already in the criticism of her, that is both affectionate and at the same time rather puzzled, how difficult the directors of the Kirov were finding it to establish an extreme individualist within a company with such a long, and, in some ways, so static a tradition.

Makarova speaks with great affection of her teachers at the Kirov who did not attempt to force their ideas upon her, but allowed her as free an expression of her intuitive vision as was possible within the rigid framework of Soviet dogma in relation to the arts. It is difficult for us in the West to understand this: for any country to lay down as a kind of moral law that only one form of artistic expression is permissible—especially one so dubious as Socialist Realism—seems quite absurd. I shall deal with this later, but it is sufficient to say at this point that a Communist party bureaucrat, who may well be entirely ignorant of the ballet, or, indeed, of any art form, has the power to close a production, and, indeed, to interfere with it during its creation. I think far more credit should be given to the Director of the Kirov—at that time Konstantin Sergeyev—and his leading teacher, Natalia Dudinskaya, in that they encouraged the individuality of this brilliant young dancer, and, as time went on, left matters of interpretation to her, advising her only on technical points. It took high courage to do this and a concern for her integrity as an artist, and I do not think Makarova herself would like this to go un-marked.

Makarova was fortunate in that her exceptional gifts were recognised by two teachers at the Kirov who exactly complemented one another. From Tatiana Vecheslova she gained a deep insight into the dance as a form of emotional expression; to her she owed much of the style, subtlety and dramatic intensity which the critics noticed so early in her career. Vecheslova was a woman of wide culture, one of a circle of poets and painters who met frequently to discuss new ideas in art and the exploration of new forms. She was thus able to see the classical dance in relationship to a wider culture than is usual in the world of the ballet which is, on the whole, limited and self-absorbed. Her first concern was to seek poetic expressiveness in movement, and to relate this to one's inner emotional life, to discover the quality in movement that would transcend the inherent limitations of the classical form. The subtlety of her mind and her intellectual curiosity were of profound value to the young dancer who questioned so deeply and sought with such eagerness for emotional truth in her art.

To balance this approach, Makarova obtained from Natalia Dudinskaya, former *prima ballerina* of the Kirov, the technical strength and the purity of classical style that were essential if she were to encompass her vision. Dudinskaya during her career had been a ballerina of phenomenal technical accomplishment, though she was seriously limited in dramatic and expressive range. Her finest part was in *Don Quixote*, a display piece of dazzling pyrotechnics, where, Makarova tells me, her dancing achieved a technical brilliance in speed, precision and balance that she has rarely seen equalled. On the other hand, in roles such as Giselle that call for great emotional range and dramatic insight, Dudinskaya was not successful. She was a pure classicist, concerned with matters of line and formal elegance of movement rather than in the dance as a means of emotional expression, thus being in direct descent from such great ballerinas of the Imperial Theatre as Kshessinska, Preobrajenska and Trefilova. She lacked Vecheslova's wide culture, but her understanding of the technical range of the classical style was of profound value to her young protégée, even though, at times, there was disagreement between them in matters of interpretation.

Dudinskaya quickly recognised what a wonderful instrument this young dancer's body was for all the demands of the classical dance; its superb proportions and her instinctive sense of line were a gift of nature for which Makarova is still profoundly grateful. Makarova often refers to this herself. In a long interview, published in *The Times*, she said recently: 'I think in all my life I never found anything easy to dance, but luckily I have the right body. That's something you are born with, either you have a right body or a wrong body for dancing, and that's why I have great respect for those who manage to make a good career with a difficult body. That can be interesting to see how they overcome difficulty, but for me, harmony is everything.'

Seeing her on the stage, one is conscious how tiny she is, with such long slender arms and legs, a combination of steel and moonlight. Photographs of her at that time show her much plumper, her arms and legs less slender, the features slightly muzzy with unawakened youth. Yet one recognises those seeking eyes—in life a dazzling blue, sometimes darkening to purple—and that expression at once alert and guarded. She is more beautiful now, and, with her fair hair cut short, she has a vivacity that one misses from the grave young woman in those early days at the Kirov.

Makarova regrets that his duties as director of the Kirov Ballet left Konstantin Sergeyev, with whom she also studied, little time to teach, as she says he is a teacher of genius and an artist of great sensibility. He has not, unfortunately, great gifts as a choreographer, and Makarova feels he has dissipated his talent in the wrong direction. As a dancer, regular partner to Ulanova, he was a superb dramatic mime and an expressive artist. Makarova, who partnered him in *Giselle* in his final performance, tells me how she will never forget his entry in the second act of the ballet, its nobility and sense of style.

All I have written about the dancing of Natalia Makarova was written before I had read the Russian critics, and it is fascinating to discover how close the ballerina of today is to that young dancer at the Kirov. We are still able to observe the same characteristics, unique to herself, in the originality of her art. These critics noticed them, and they were surprised and a little uneasy. They recognised a sense of solitude around her, hints of an extreme vulnerability. They found within her the eternal unrest of the true artist: as one of them writes, 'she searches within and this searching will never cease.' They sensed also a mood of hidden questioning, of a private apprehension. They saw her as modern, individualistic and unique: as I did in 1961, they recognised in her a potential genius.

Makarova danced the second act *pas de deux* of *Giselle* for the first time at a graduation concert at the Vaganova School in 1959, although she was not to dance the complete ballet until two years later when she gave her first performance at Covent Garden. The second act presented her with no great problems, but it was not until several years later that she was able to achieve the right dramatic balance in the first act. It takes a long time, Makarova says, for a ballerina to move from complexity to simplicity in her art, where only the essence remains and all that is unnecessary has been stripped away. It is the same, she agrees, with all great art: it is a search for that truth, spoken with the greatest simplicity, that will enclose and encompass all, as one line of poetry will contain within it a world of associations and profound resonances. This she seeks in her dancing, but it is attained only after years of refinement and compression in the imagery of the dance.

Even if we feel some of the Russian critics were oddly insensitive, one can understand their dilemma: here, in her first great role, Makarova did not conform; she took her own way, followed her own intuitions, and this was not seemly in so young a dancer. The Kirov has, after all, the longest and most noble tradition of any ballet company in the world, and it is right that this should be so regarded. What they attributed to her stubbornness and extreme individuality was, in fact, due only to inexperience that led her to over-decorate the ballet with too much detail, so that it lacked the divine simplicity of Ulanova's interpretation which Makarova was herself later to encompass in the role.

For me it was the acute sensitivity to the Romantic period and to its line, brought about by a study of the lithographs of the period, that made the greatest impression when I saw her dance the role at that first performance at Covent Garden in 1961. It was a revelation in style of which, over many previous years, I had only caught glimpses in the performances of Western ballerinas, and it was as a result of this that I began to find in the classical dance a new world of movement, far greater in expressiveness than any I had previously known. It was tentative, exploratory; yet, even incomplete, it was flawless, like a half-opened rose that awaits the fullness of the day. The source of this book is that first performance of Natalia Makarova in *Giselle*.

It was at another of these graduation concerts, also in 1959, that Makarova first attempted the role of Odette. At first she was not truly successful. She had yet to discover how the icy classicism of the *danse d'école* could be related to characterisation. It seems she felt imprisoned within it, so that the freedom of interpretation she had found in the Romanticism of Perrot was not so easily won in the classicism of Petipa and Ivanov. She was not content to dance the role solely in terms of line and phrasing, yet at the same time the restriction of the form did not seem to allow her sufficient dramatic scope.

I think, in fact, that *Swan Lake* is a far more difficult ballet than *Giselle* for the ballerina, and it takes many years for her to achieve not only the reconciliation within the double role, but also the dramatic freedom allowed to her in the academic dance. It was not until 1974 and 1975 that Makarova was finally able to achieve this balance, and to give the double role her own individuality and insight. Most ballerinas never reach this point: they remain throughout their careers content with the traditional playing of the role, particularly in the third act, which is why Makarova's present interpretation has come as a revelation, a new discovery in the classical dance. In her early days at the Kirov she was content to play Odile as the evil enchantress, unrelated to Odette, and though in her early photographs she looks delightfully seductive (but less beautiful than she is today) one is not surprised to find her now very scornful at the naivety of such an interpretation.

It is strange to learn from Makarova that it was not until her last two years at the Vaganova School, from 1957 until her graduation to the Kirov Ballet in 1959, that she became seriously dedicated to her life as a dancer. Before that she had been interested, but not deeply engaged, and the consciousness of her gifts only became apparent to her very late in her training. Yet she moved straight into principal roles with the Company without having to serve any long apprenticeship in the *corps de ballet*, which is very unusual, particularly in a Russian Company, where the training is longer and more thorough than any given in the West. In this her career continued to follow that of Anna Pavlova, even to a repetition of the same event when each ballerina fell into the prompter's box at one of her first performances.

One of her first major roles was that of Maria in *The Fountain of Bakhchisarai*, a ballet with choreography by Rostislav Zakharov, based on a poem by Pushkin, to music by Asafiev. The part had been created by Galina Ulanova, who was the choreographer's original inspiration, and it became one of her most famous roles. In an article published in the magazine *Teatr* in 1949, Ulanova has many fascinating things to say about her interpretation, one of which in particular brings us very close to the art of her successor. Ulanova writes:

With the years my Maria seemed to come to life. The pattern of the role became more complicated, the character of the heroine acquired more facets. New smiles, new expressiveness of the arms, new linear *plastique* were found for her. I think in the end I succeeded in finding in my Maria, that state of calm, so necessary for any actor, when all the nuances of the image become quite organic.

41

Makarova never saw Ulanova dance, but of course her performance in *The Fountain of Bakhchisarai* was already legendary when she graduated into the Company. Yet, once again, she took her own line; this Maria was to be very different. Ulanova was soft, poetic and yielding; yet with Makarova, according to a contemporary critic, 'one could hear the insistent beat of an impatient, demanding and stubborn heart.' Her Maria did not accept her fate; she defied it. When she was captured and brought to Guirei's harem, Ulanova accepted all with a quiet resignation. Not so the young Makarova: neither temperamentally nor artistically would she accept anything. The same critic writes: 'If Ulanova dies as a sensitive plant, Makarova protests to the very end.' An interesting side-light on this review, that shows how consistent the ballerina has been in her interpretations, is the remark that Makarova seemed in some way to become attracted to her brutal captor, and to react in a manner towards him that might be acceptable to this type of person.

I was reminded of this when discussing with Makarova her role of the Black Queen in Ninette de Valois' *Checkmate*, when she was learning the part before her first London performances in October 1975. Here, Makarova told me, was a person who sought to entrap and destroy the Red Knight, but at the same time felt for him a growing attraction and a curious sense of compassion. She began to love him, even as she sought to destroy him. This is, of course, the reverse of her attitude in *The Fountain of Bakhchisarai*, but here again one sees the subtlety of her imagination that can see attraction, or even love, within a context of the deepest hostility. This is a consistent attitude of hers, and, as we shall see in a later chapter, has had a profound influence on her playing of Odile in *Swan Lake*. The fact that she played to Guirei in a manner to which his personality would respond is also a constant feature of her approach to a role, and I shall deal with this in much greater detail when I come to discuss her views on the relationship between the ballerina and her partner.

Modern Russian ballet (I do not use the term Soviet Ballet, since this is a political misnomer, implying some sort of revolutionary break with the past) is not so ossified as one might imagine from the repertoire of the Bolshoi and Kirov companies when they come to London. It is insular, complacent even, shackled by the demands of Socialist Realism, out of touch with developments in modern choreography and music, yet it has produced its own choreographers and developed its own style. Of these choreographers, one of the most remarkable was Leonid Yacobson, for many years principal choreographer to the Kirov Ballet, who died in 1975. Makarova speaks of his work with great admiration, and still remembers the excitement of having roles created for her by him.

Yacobson graduated from the Kirov school in 1926. His choreography had been profoundly influenced by the ideas of Michel Fokine and Isadora Duncan. Indeed he continued to create dances for the Isadora Duncan studio in Moscow, which had been maintained by her former pupils, until 1949. His initial studies, coupled with the influence of the Vaganova method, led him to produce works in highly different styles, whose common element was a profound sense of *plastique*.

As a choreographer Yacobson was in some ways in the autocratic tradition of Petipa; he had an exact idea of the ballet he was to create in his mind, so that the dancers had initially little to contribute to its creation. They had, Makarova tells me, to take his ideas on trust and commit themselves entirely to his vision, even before they had grasped it as a whole. Yet he shared the same gift as many great choreographers in being able to find within the personality of the dancer a potential of which she herself would be entirely unaware. In Makarova's questioning and troubled inner world he found a new source of inspiration, and she has little doubt that he has had a profound influence on her later development as a dramatic ballerina.

It was for the young dancers who appeared in his ballets by no means easy to make the transition from 'turned-in' movements to the classical 'turn-out' required from them in class. Among her teachers at the Kirov there were those who felt anxious in case her work with Yacobson would seriously impede her development as a classical ballerina, and certainly she was for this reason faced with more difficult technical problems than those usually encountered by a young dancer who appears in modern works that are, on the whole, usually more orientated towards the academic technique.

Over the decade from 1960 until 1970 Yacobson created a number of roles for Makarova. One of the most original of his ballets was *The Bug*, created in 1962 and based on the satirical play of Vladimir Mayakovsky, the greatest of the post-revolutionary poets. Working to a jazz score, Yacobson created a ballet of great originality, full of grotesque movement and startling images. Playing the role of Zoya, a working girl, Makarova was the pivot round which the whole ballet turned. One critic writes of her performance that she develops from the character of a faceless doll into 'a ravaged and wrecked individual'. The music by Voznesdrenzky, to a rock and roll beat, contained moments of great pathos, leading to a tragic climax when Zoya hangs herself. For me the ballet is memorable for its beautiful scenario, written in the programme: 'Somewhere, it does not matter in what great city, there can be a solitary street lamp, a fence, a bench, and abandoned Zoya. It does not matter by whom.' *The Bug* was, indeed, one of the first roles created for Makarova that helped the young ballerina to become the great dramatic dancer we know today.

In the following year, 1963, Makarova appeared in Yacobson's ballet *Ravel Waltzes*. Set in the style of the Second Empire, the work was a study of different aspects of love, in certain ways dealing with the same themes as the later ballets of Jerome Robbins. In the second waltz, partnered by Selutsky, Makarova portrayed a woman who was both sensual and indifferent, giving herself the first opportunity to display the sophistication of her dancing that was to be seen later in the West in *Elite Syncopations*.

44

It was these same qualities she was to reveal when she first danced in Sergeyev's *Cinderella*, being given originally the part of one of the ugly sisters which by a nice irony were always danced by the most attractive girls in the Company. Here the critics noted again her modernism and sophistication. One critic writes that she might have been taken for 'a modern young lady on the deck of her own yacht, drinking a cocktail at the bar, or waiting for her flight at an international airport.'

Certainly I recall her brilliance in this role when she first danced it at Covent Garden, although its modernity did not strike me in quite this manner. I remember the daring risks she took with the musical phrases, the kind of shimmering elegance she gave to each *enchaînement*. From a ballerina for many years out of touch with contemporary influences in the dance, it was extraordinary to see a performance so chic, presented with a kind of mocking humour that exactly matched the score. If she did not make me think of cocktails and airports—and, indeed, how charmingly old-fashioned this idea of sophistication is!—she gave to the role a sly, glancing wit that I had only seen before from Renée Jeanmaire. In the midst of so stereotyped a production it glittered, diamond-pointed and incongruously bright. I could not think how she had found this within such conventional choreography; now that I know better the astounding range of her dancing and the vividness of her imagination, I would no longer be surprised, since it was something she had found in the music of which the other dancers of the Kirov were not aware.

In the role of Cinderella herself, which she first danced a year after the role of the ugly sister, Makarova was not given the same opportunities. What she created though was a unity, for this Cinderella, even from our first sight of her, was potentially already the joyous girl at her first ball; her transformation was not magic but fulfilment, the realisation of that potential for happiness that was only half-veiled in the poor, bullied child of the early scenes. This ability to see a role as a developing unity is, of course, one of her most pronounced characteristics as a ballerina, and I shall discuss this in a later chapter when I come to consider her dancing in more detail.

At the end of 1975 Makarova was to dance the part again in Frederick Ashton's ballet, so much more finely drawn and rich in expressive choreography, where she was to glitter, like a frosted star, against the music. In a sense with this performance she had come a full circle, established with the Royal Ballet in her true artistic home.

In 1965 she won the gold medal at the international dance competition in Varna, an honour she shares with her fellow artist, Mikhail Baryshnikov, who also defected from the Kirov Ballet. In 1970 she was awarded the Pavlova prize. I understand that their names have been deleted from the roll of honour at Varna; if this is true, it is an act of pettiness and political spite for which the authorities there should be ashamed. It is, however, extraordinary that, in less than twelve years from graduation into the Kirov Ballet, she should have won the two greatest individual prizes in the world of ballet. Even if this is no longer recorded in Varna, it is recorded here.

Of all her roles at the Kirov, Makarova speaks with the most enthusiasm about the part of the Beautiful Maiden in Yacobson's *Country of Wonder* which he created for her in 1967. This ballet on the horrors and futilities of war is based on highly-stylised and abbreviated movement, at times grotesque, at others full of compassion. From what Makarova has told me (for this ballet has never been seen in the West) it must bear some resemblance to Kurt Jooss' great work, *The Green Table*, and possibly to the section 'Mars' in Tudor's ballet, *The Planets*. The role he created for her was central to the entire work, and from photographs one can gain a very clear insight into the originality of his ideas.

During her years at the Kirov, Makarova danced as well as *Giselle* and *Swan Lake*, all the ballerina roles—in *Raymonda*, *The Sleeping Beauty* which she first danced in 1968, *The Hump-backed Horse*, and in

Lavrovsky's famous version of *Romeo and Juliet*. In this ballet she was criticised in some quarters for modern touches she brought to the choreography and for the strength and passionate realism of her interpretation, which was compared, unfavourably, with Ulanova's more simple and lyrical approach. It is, however, interesting that these critics were deeply in sympathy with the freshness of insight she gave to these traditional roles, even to the point of complaining that she was not allowed sufficient scope to develop so original a vision. It was, of course, this sense of being cramped artistically, given too few roles in which she could develop her own style, that finally decided Makarova to leave the Kirov Ballet in 1970. No one was more conscious than her of this wasted potential, no ballerina more eager to stretch her imagination to limits far beyond those set by old-fashioned choreography, even if she was not yet to know to what distant frontiers this was to lead her in the mysterious discoveries of her art.

# THREE

# *The Ballerina*

As BALLERINA of the Kirov Makarova was among a privileged
elite in the Soviet Union. For dancing leading roles, perhaps only
four or five times a month, she was paid by Soviet standards an
enormous salary—some 350 roubles, about a third more than that
given to a skilled workman or a member of the managerial classes.
She had her own flat. This may not seem much to us in the West,
but, such is the shortage of accommodation in the Soviet Union, to
own your flat is a rare luxury. She held the title of 'Honoured Artist
of the Russian Federation', and would, no doubt, in time have been
awarded the highest tribute, that of 'People's Artist'. Above all, she
was able to travel abroad. This, though it may appear a commonplace to us, is the rarest privilege granted in the Soviet Union,
usually only offered to respected figures of the Communist party,
or to members of its various delegations who visit the West.

Makarova was never a member of the Communist Party, and no
pressure was put upon her to join. In some respects this was not help-
ful to her career in terms of promotion but her abilities were so great
that it was impossible they should go unrecognised. Indeed she kept
herself free of all political activities, finding it safer when dealing
with those of authority within the Party to act the role of an empty-
headed ballet girl to whom the intricacies of dialectical materialism
were quite beyond her comprehension. Her brilliant intellect and
avid curiosity she hid to such good effect that, although she was

Aged fourteen
and a recent portrait study

*Swan Lake* (American Ballet Theatre)

deeply upset and ashamed by such events as the Soviet invasion of Czechoslovakia, she kept her council and concentrated on her *pirouettes*. She was never considered a security risk within the Company, adequately infiltrated by members of the Communist party to whose authorities any such deviations would be reported. No one in the Kirov Company, even the closest friends, even talked about the possibility of defecting to the West; they would not dare to do so.

Apart from the political pressure to which all artists in the Soviet Union are subjected, she was also the victim of a kind of aesthetic puritanism of which we in the West can have little comprehension. The ideals of Socialist Realism in Soviet aesthetics are not one of many theories about the nature of art; they are the sole criterion upon which any work is to be judged, whether in literature, painting or the dance. Briefly this philosophy can be described as one in which the ideals of Soviet Communism must dictate both the form and the content of a work of art in any media which will thus have its own social purpose.

As the finest ambassadors of Soviet culture the dancers were most closely watched for any deviation from this ideal. It could not be defied, except at grave risk to one's career. For a ballerina of such imaginative resources, anxious always to extend the range of her art, the continual interference by the Communist party in matters of free expression became increasingly irksome. Makarova had no wish to spend her entire career dancing in the traditional ballets; she was eager for experiment, avid for new ideas. She recalls how Leonid Yacobson, a most respected and important figure in the Company, ran into difficulties on several occasions. He attempted to create one ballet based on the life of Mary Magdalen, but this was forbidden on anti-religious grounds. Another attempt to compose dances inspired by Picasso, in which Makarova danced the leading role, was banned because the images were grotesque and considered decadent. Makarova recalls how, after the first performance of this role, she had a telephone call from an official at the Smolny headquarters of the Leningrad Communist party. He asked her mildly what she thought of the ballet, and when she replied that it was interesting to perform and contained many unusual and striking images, he began to cast doubts on the value of the work, describing it as ugly and uninspiring. At the end of the conversation he advised her (informally, of course, and as a friend and admirer of her work) not to perform it any more. The ballet was never danced again.

Makarova had another experience, very similar to that of Yacobson in his Picasso ballet, when she agreed to work on a new version of *Romeo and Juliet*, to music by Berlioz, with choreography by her friend and colleague, Igor Tchernichov. She admired the work; to her it seemed original and full of fresh ideas in movement, so that she devoted all her free time during one season to working on it with the young choreographer. When the ballet was completed it was shown in rehearsal to the party officials, and was turned down flat as being erotic and decadent; indeed they made it clear that the choreographer was himself a rebel against accepted Socialist standards in art. It was, in fact, danced just once at a special performance given by Irina Kolpakova, a respected ballerina and a devoted member of the Communist party. Even with her backing it was never given a second performance. Makarova would perform in it again, many years later as we shall see, but under circumstances of which she would never have dreamed in those early years with the Kirov.

The ideological pressures on the dancers were continuous; at every meeting of the Company to discuss future works there would be the same call for new, socialist ballets. The basis for the repertoire, however, remained the old ballets of the nineteenth century, part of the Company's inheritance from the past. Some of the senior ballerinas, such as Kolpakova, were content to face a future dancing only in these works, but Makarova was restless. She had seen Western ballet on the various tours of the Kirov abroad, and had been struck by a choreographic range far beyond anything she was able to discover in the Soviet Union. She longed to dance in ballets by Ashton, Tudor and Robbins, to work with new forms, develop further aspects of her talent. Her three seasons in London gave her particular delight, for she came to love the city where she had built up a large and vociferous public, to make her the most popular ballerina of the Kirov Company. It was a disappointment to them that she was seen in so few roles outside the classics that taxed her to any real extent.

I recall how, before the final performance at Covent Garden for the 1964 season, a petition to the Director of the Company was organised by a group of ballet enthusiasts asking that she should dance in something other than a dreary little piece called *The Blind Girl*, one of Yacobson's less successful efforts. I remember also how, during the same season, after her last performance in *Giselle*, she was surrounded by a large crowd at the stage door who followed her, clapping and cheering, down the length of Floral Street.

Some of the dancers and choreographers at the Kirov, impatient with the official attitude to their work and the incessant demands for Socialist Realist ballets, decided to form their own, experimental dance group. This was to be rather on the lines of the early Ballet Rambert in England, an attempt at chamber ballet, incorporating music from all periods. The choreography was entrusted to a talented young man, Georgi Alexidze, and he gathered together a small group of dancers, together with musicians from the Leningrad Philharmonic Orchestra.

At first officialdom smiled on the venture, but then Makarova danced in a new work, entitled *Ave Maria*. It received one performance, and then was dropped from the repertoire. Two years later she was asked to dance it again, then to find that the title had been changed to *Anonymous: 16th Century*.

The third visit of the Kirov Ballet to London in the summer of 1970 was in many ways its least happy one. The Festival Hall where they appeared is not good for ballet: the stage is small and shallow, with room neither to hang the scenery nor to give the dancers any space within the wings, while the surface is hard and unyielding. The dancers found it unnerving to dance with out any proscenium, and were in constant dread lest one too wide *jeté* was going to carry them into the orchestra pit. Apart from *Giselle*, they were unable to present the nineteenth century classics, and the programmes had to be filled with *divertissements* that gave the public no real idea of the collective strength of the Company. As well as *Giselle*, in which she shared the title role with Kolpakova and Sizova, Makarova appeared in *Chopiniana* and Dolin's *Pas de Quatre*, and also in various *pas de deux*.

Although she was warmly received by the public, one could sense that Makarova was not happy to dance under these circumstances, yet the three performances she gave in *Giselle* had an agonised intensity that was a startling advance on anything she had previously danced in London. Even when she appeared in only a single item, one felt that each step was being danced with a new passion, so that the familiar Blue Bird *pas de deux* took on a kind of throbbing urgency, and was shaped with so fastidious a concern for line that it burned with all the brilliance of a sapphire; dancing that lay like a string of jewels across the stage. In a note I had from her towards the end of the season I got this same sense of dissatisfaction, although it was contained only in a reference to the irregularities of casting, so that it was difficult, even for her, to know what she would be dancing over the coming week. We met briefly after her last performance in *Giselle*, when I noticed how tired and strained she looked.

On the day she left the Company, Makarova attended a lunch at the Soviet Embassy. There she spoke freely about the lack of new roles and the limitations this placed upon her as an artist. It was true that she was already preparing for the role of Ophelia in a new ballet on *Hamlet* to be danced at the Kirov the following season, but after that she could only see a succession of Giselles and Odettes stretching before her. She had been to the American Ballet Theatre who were appearing at the same time at Covent Garden, and must have been aware, even though the season was not a successful one, how much more a Western company would have to offer her. Yet at that time she had no thought at all of defecting. She had bought a car which was to be shipped over to the Soviet Union for her; indeed she still keeps the receipt for her deposit as a souvenir. One imagined that this was a sort of decoy to keep the Soviets off her track but it was not so; she fully intended to return with the Company at the end of that week and make what she could of the limitations that constricted her.

That evening she dined with friends. Conversation turned on the subject of ballet in the Soviet Union, and suddenly quite on an impulse, with no prior consideration, yet now without any doubts, she decided to stay in the West. A friend telephoned the local police station and explained the circumstances. Very shortly afterwards two policemen arrived in a police car—'A very nice contrast they were to the N.K.V.D.' Makarova told me. While her application for political asylum was being considered at the Home Office she remained in the station. She could speak no English, and she was too excited and nervous to sleep, having always in her mind the terrible fear that her application would be refused. The police made her innumerable cups of tea, smiled at her encouragingly and tried some disjointed conversation, while she smoked one cigarette after another. Yet she felt no doubts: what she had done, she knew, was the right thing for her as an artist; now it became obvious to her, and she has not in the years that have followed ever doubted the rightness of this decision. The following day she received confirmation from the Home Office that her application had been granted, and at once she went into hiding at a friend's home in the country.

# FOUR

# *In the West*

~~~~~~~~~~

ON FRIDAY, 5th September, 1970 the news of Natalia Makarova's defection from the Kirov Ballet broke across the front pages of all the papers in a clamour of raucous headlines. The stories varied quite considerably in detail, the most popular version being that she had walked out of the Strand Palace Hotel where the company had been staying, and was not seen again. In more dramatic reports she leaped into a waiting car. There were photographs of the ballerina, and one resourceful cameraman had obtained a picture of her abandoned dressing room at the Festival Hall with flowers and ballet shoes artfully arranged. It did, as a matter of fact, look rather different from the room in which I had seen her two nights previously, but the intention was there.

The explanation for her leaving the Kirov Ballet was taken by the press to be a romantic one, since they obviously felt that so grave a decision could hardly have been made for artistic reasons. The Administrative Director of the Kirov Ballet, Pyotr Rachinsky, hinted darkly that the ballerina must obviously have been under some very strong pressures, leaving the matter to settle uneasily there. After a telephone conversation with the Foreign Secretary, Sir Alec Douglas-Home, Mr. Smirnovsky, the Soviet Ambassador, later met Sir Denis Greenhill of the Foreign Office. The ballerina refused to speak to officials from the Soviet Embassy who attempted through the Foreign Office to get in touch with her.

On Saturday, 6th September, the Kirov Company gave their last performance at the Festival Hall, flying the next day to Holland where they were engaged to appear. The storm subsided, leaving the last word to a rather sour editorial in the *Daily Telegraph* which concluded: 'Everyone who escapes from the Soviet Union has committed a political act, even if it was only dislike of cabbage soup which caused it.'

A few days later Makarova was interviewed on television in the programme '24 Hours'. She repeated once again that her decision had been made solely for artistic reasons, adding, 'I had to summon up all my courage to leave my mother, my friends and my Company. I really can't bear to talk about it.' Since that first interview she has been asked the same questions again and again over the last seven years, and in this respect I have been another of the offenders, although I never doubted her integrity as an artist and her deep concern for the truths of her art which made her decision the only logical one to follow.

Immediately after her defection she received a large number of letters from members of the Kirov Company begging her to return. Some were from her close friends, and were obviously sincere and written in perplexity and true feeling, but others were stereotyped, all in the same stilted language, that made her sure they had been composed as a result of a directive from the Company. The Artistic Director of the Kirov, Konstantin Sergeyev, aslo wrote with genuine affection and concern, asking her to consider her decision in the light of her artistic career. Makarova has always had a deep respect and admiration for Sergeyev, but she had to reply that as an artist he could understand better than anyone else why she had felt obliged to make such a decision. Then she was free. A new creative life opened before her, one that she had not in any way prepared for herself, but which she awaited with that strange blend of fatalism and trust that is so much a part of her character.

In a letter to me, written when she was at her country retreat,

Makarova said how much she longed to dance before her London public again, but sadly this was not to be for over two years. This must have been a great disappointment to her, since she loves London where she has made her home, and has great respect for the taste and judgment of the London ballet public.

After leaving the Kirov Makarova was first seen on television, where she danced the *pas de deux* from the third act of *Swan Lake* partnered by Rudolf Nureyev. The appearance of the two former Kirov dancers drew a great deal of publicity, though a virtuoso *pas de deux*, stripped of its dramatic context, did not display her to the best advantage. Curiously enough, though she and Nureyev had sometimes been in the same ballets at the Kirov, they had never danced together before. It did not seem likely that they would now form a regular partnership, since Nureyev's famous partnership with Dame Margot Fonteyn was well established. It was, however, an interesting contrast in style and personality.

Shortly after this it was announced that Makarova had accepted an invitation to join the American Ballet Theatre as a regular member of the Company. Ballet Theatre has the widest repertoire of modern ballets of any large-scale company in the world, and together with these it presents revivals of *Swan Lake*, *Giselle*, *Coppélia* and the traditional version of *La Fille mal gardée*. As such it seemed to offer Makarova the right balance of modern, classical and experimental roles in which to extend her artistic scope. In fact many of the works in which she danced were unworthy of her, and did not offer sufficient challenge to her gifts, while, at the same time, she felt the lack of artistic guidance which would have been invaluable in this unfamiliar world.

The range of dance activities in New York is wider than London, since the modern and free dance are much more firmly established, due to the influence of Martha Graham, Merce Cunningham and others. It was exactly this range of experiment, the sense of an openness to all creative ideas, however unexpected or bizarre, the eclecticism of the dance world, that most impressed Makarova when she came to work in the United States. Here was a complete contrast to the ballet scene in the Soviet Union, so rigid in its aesthetics, so narrow in its concept of the dance, an environment in which she could experiment and move freely until she had become acclimatised to Western ballet.

She worked very hard, with far more performances than she had ever been expected to dance in the Soviet Union, but this was of considerable value in terms of technique and stamina. In addition, her engagement with Ballet Theatre gave her an opportunity to dance in works by Antony Tudor, at that time—and, alas, also at present—quite inadequately represented by the Royal Ballet. Makarova was promised that new works would be created around her, but these did not, in fact, materialise apart from an isolated *pas de deux*. Unfortunately also the productions of the classical ballets of the nineteenth century both in the quality of dancing and in sense of style were far inferior to those at the Kirov.

Her engagement with Ballet Theatre also allowed her a chance to fulfil one of her first ambitions—to dance with Erik Bruhn, at that time undoubtedly the finest male dancer in the Western world. Since then his career has been sadly marred by illness, though it gave her great delight when he returned to partner her in a *pas de deux*, created for them by John Neumeier in 1975.

The first performance she gave with Ballet Theatre was at a special gala on 24th December, 1970, at the City Centre where she appeared in *Giselle*. Erik Bruhn who was to have partnered her was taken ill, being replaced at very short notice by Ivan Nagy who later became her regular partner. The house was crammed, and the tension on both sides of the curtain enormous; but at the end the audience rose to her, and the press was equally enthusiastic. It was interesting that more than one critic compared her dancing to that of Alicia Markova whose interpretation of Giselle had become so famous when she danced during the war years with Ballet Theatre, though certainly I have rarely seen two great ballerinas so different in style.

For the following season with Ballet Theatre early in 1971 Makarova was partnered by Erik Bruhn in *Giselle* at the Lincoln Center, also appearing in the traditional version of *La Fille mal gardée* and in *Coppélia*. She had never seen *Coppélia* performed on the stage, so that she was able to make something quite new of Swanilda. In this, her first real comic role, she achieved wonders of zany fun, a series of brilliant jokes within the traditional choreography that combined both wit and knock-about farce. She tended to vary her effects as the mood took her, though certain passages of mime and by-play remained constant, and her dancing had an air of improvisation about it, like a series of sudden witticisms made up on the spur of the moment. One regrets that she has not danced this role in Europe, as it would afford a glimpse of an entirely new aspect of her genius, but at the moment she is tired of it, even to the extent of saying she cannot bear to listen to its enchanting music any more. However there is nothing final about her attitude to her roles; maybe once again with the Royal Ballet she may be caught up in the music's airy brilliance, and respond anew to that most child-like and entrancing of all old ballets.

To protect herself from routine performances in this ballet she would improvise new humorous effects each time. Once, she recalls, after the final *pas de deux* in the third act, when she had indulged herself in some particularly long balances, she found herself crippled with a violent cramp in the legs. 'It was,' she says, 'God punishing me for indulging in over-long balances'. This sad news she whispered to her partner, who with great presence of mind when they were due to dance again picked her up and carried her across the stage. So frantic, affronted and astonished were her mime and gestures at this point that the audience roared with laughter, many of them thinking that this was part of the traditional choreography. She tried to repeat the effect at the next performance but it did not work again.

The version of *La Fille mal gardée*, presented by Ballet Theatre, is, Makarova agrees, far inferior to Ashton's reworked ballet both in choreography and characterisation. It does, however, provide the ballerina with a great deal of rather obvious virtuoso dancing, sufficient for her to illuminate it with her own elegance and dazzling technique. One is reminded of Anna Pavlova, that magical alchemist of the dance, who could transform the scraps of such old ballets into images flawless as gold.

In that season Makarova also appeared for the first time in Antony Tudor's *Lilac Garden*, that exquisite evocation of defeated love, set in the long twilight of a summer day, where the heart cracks beneath the social façade, and breaks, unnoticed, in the fading hour. Nowhere in the history of the modern dance has the slow unfolding of hidden grief been more poignantly displayed, where each pose is like a broken sigh, a world of abiding recollections caught in images of the most desolating beauty.

It is not surprising that this great work, composed by Tudor for the young dancers of Ballet Rambert in 1936, took him six months to create, since there is within it not a single step or gesture that does not speak in truth, even to the most secret longings of the heart. It is unusual in that it is balanced by two contrasting female roles—the bride-to-be, Caroline, caught in a marriage of convenience who tries so desperately to say farewell to her lover, and her fiancé's mistress who will not be set aside. Makarova's interpretation of Caroline has become one of her greatest achievements in expressive dance, showing us an anguish barely controlled by the social conventions in which she moves, a fierce desolation, made more poignant for being so briefly seen or frozen into moments of an absolute stillness, as if her tears glimmered but did not fall. At this stage in her career she would like to alternate in the two roles, and, as the ballet has been in the repertoire of the Royal Ballet, one hopes that she will be given this opportunity further to extend her range and our understanding of this great work.

59

Tudor was fascinated to work with Makarova, not only because she was the first Kirov-trained dancer to appear in his ballets, but also because her concern to find emotional truth within the dance exactly matched his own view of choreography which he sees purely in dramatic and emotional terms. They communicated through the dance itself, since she could speak no English. It was a difficult time for her, as she was learning several new works, so that in desperation she asked Tudor to come round to her flat one evening and coach her individually in the role of Caroline. She remembers how he danced the whole ballet for her on the sitting-room carpet.

Makarova tells me that Tudor prefers his dancers not to be too sure how to interpret a role when it comes to performance, since he feels he obtains a truer response if they seek themselves for its inner quality as they dance it. This, he believes, brings to the performance a greater emotional impact and a more personal approach than would be the case if they were already certain they understood the character and the emotional quality of each *enchaînement*. She cannot, however, work in this manner, so that before she danced the role of Caroline she had thought very deeply into the nature of the character and the situation in which she was involved. Here there is not for her any identification with an imaginary person, but a discovery within herself of her own emotions were she to be confronted with the identical situation.

This highly personal approach to a role must have intrigued Tudor, for he would give her no indication beyond the steps themselves how he wished it to be performed; indeed when she came to learn *Dark Elegies* in 1972, she was not at first even aware that the dancers were peasant women until she began to sense this in the heavy quality of movement and made judicious inquiries from her colleagues. It seems that Tudor was anxious that she should find her own truth in his ballets, maybe one from which he would be able to learn himself. With dancers of exceptional gifts—as Tudor had found earlier with Nora Kaye—new meanings will be discovered within the dance of which the choreographer himself was possibly unaware. One is reminded of T. S. Eliot who, when asked what certain passages in his poems meant, would refer the inquirer to Helen Gardner who, he said, understood them better than he did.

Another new role was *La Sylphide* which she danced in the same season with Erik Bruhn. Here she had the inestimable advantage of appearing with a great dancer, himself trained by the Royal Danish Ballet who are the true guardians of the work, and he had much to teach her about the tradition of Bournonville where the softer, more rounded movements of the Franco-Danish school are so different from the Russian style formed by Petipa. It was historically right that she should, in 1974, dance the role at the Theatre Royal in Copenhagen, on this occasion partnered by Mikhail Baryshnikov. I watched those performances, bewitching in their evocation of the sly, mocking Sylphide, as delicate and evanescent as a pale rose, a kind of Victorian miniature painted fastidiously on the air.

At the end of this, her first full season with Ballet Theatre, Makarova went on tour with the Company, dancing in Los Angeles, Chicago (where she had danced in her first *Sleeping Beauty* with the Kirov in 1968) and San Francisco. Then she returned for a further season at the Lincoln Centre.

During this season Alvin Ailey created a new section for his ballet *The River* as a *pas de deux* for her and Erik Bruhn. It was not very distinguished as choreography, but it gave her an opportunity to dance to jazz music by Duke Ellington. Another work new to her was a version of *The Miraculous Mandarin*, to music by Bartok, by the Swedish choreographer, Ulf Gadd, a ballet also of no great distinction which did not survive for long in the repertoire.

Makarova's first engagement with the Royal Ballet in London was to be at a gala performance, attended by the Queen Mother, in the summer of 1972. She looked forward to this enormously, and it was a cruel disappointment that a leg injury, sustained at the dress rehearsal of the *pas de deux* from the third act of *Swan Lake* where she was partnered by Rudolf Nureyev, led to her withdrawal from the programme. Previously she had given her first guest performance in *Giselle* with the Royal Swedish Ballet to which she was to return the following year. One of her happiest memories of this visit was her meeting with Ingmar Bergman, whose films she has always greatly admired, and the great director was equally fascinated by her performances, seeing in them the dramatic intensity for which he aims in his own creations. A further coast-to-coast tour with Ballet Theatre followed, also a guest performance with the PACT Ballet in Johannesberg.

During the autumn of 1972 Makarova danced her first performances with the Royal Ballet at Covent Garden, appearing in *Swan Lake* and *Giselle*. Since she had last appeared in London with the Kirov Ballet her style had been broadened and enriched, drawn with a far greater amplitude of movement and an increased subtlety of musical thought. Those who had prophesied that her departure from the Kirov would result in a technical decline were confounded.

It was after this season that she decided to resign as a permanent member of Ballet Theatre, although she would continue to dance with them as a guest artist but for a limited number of performances only. After two years she felt it was time to widen her experience by appearing with many different companies; also she was disappointed that no new roles had been created for her by Ballet Theatre, as she had been promised, and the situation did not seem likely to improve. From then onwards she travelled the world, dancing in Rome, Milan, Turin, Oslo, Stockholm, Zurich, Berlin and Paris, as well as making guest appearances with Ballet Theatre. She also danced for a season in Australia. She appeared several times with the Ballet Company at La Scala, Milan where she danced the Chosen Maiden in John Taras' version of *The Rite of Spring*. This role was perhaps the most taxing of her career, since her final solo lasted five minutes, equalling in its demands on stamina and technique the famous solo designed by Massine in his version of the ballet for Lydia Sokolova, of which she has given a memorable account in her book, *Dancing for Diaghilev*. Also in Italy, at Turin, she appeared in Maria Callas' production of *Sicilian Vespers* where the choreography was by Serge Lifar.

This was the first time she had worked with Lifar with whom she established a relationship based on mutual trust and admiration. Whatever doubts one may have of his gifts as a choreographer, Lifar's wealth of experience and the force of his personality made a profound effect upon Makarova, an artist deeply conscious of the great traditions of her art. After these performances he gave her a present of a signed portrait, addressed to 'The Stradivarius of the Dance'.

She returned to the Royal Ballet in 1973 to make her first appearance in *Romeo and Juliet*, a role that remains, together with *Manon* the greatest achievement to date of her artistic career. In her dancing the poetry and music were reconciled with a lyrical intensity, a richness of nuance and a nobility of style she had never achieved before. In the balcony scene she so transcended the limitations of the classical style that her dancing burned with a kind of elemental fire in an ecstatic communion with the music. Here one saw not just a young girl in love, but the very spirit of love itself, set deep within the throbbing heart of the music. It was up to that point the crown of her life's endeavours, the great flowering of her genius.

During this season she also danced Aurora in *The Sleeping Beauty*. It is not a role for which she has the same feeling as that for *Giselle* and *Swan Lake*, since it seems to her to lack real emotional development, but her dancing in the first act had a child-like radiance, while in the Vision scene she achieved an absolute purity of classical style that must have made older ballet-goers remember the dancing of Olga Spessivtzeva, the formal perfection of whose movements is now a legend in the history of the classical dance. I feel that Aurora is a role to which she may return later, and that these first performances were no more than a sketch for a richer design.

In the summer of 1973 Makarova accepted an invitation to dance in *Swan Lake*, partnered by Rudolf Nureyev, with the Paris Opéra Ballet in open air performances in the courtyard of the Louvre. These were marred by the atrocious weather—it poured with rain during two entire performances—and also by the fact that she was unwell, suffering from a displaced vertebra in the neck, dancing her last performance against her doctor's advice. The season was also marred by a much-publicised dispute between herself and Rudolf Nureyev, now happily and amicably resolved.

Upon her return from Paris Makarova was not able to dance for several weeks while her injury was treated. She then went on a short tour with the Philadelphia Ballet, returning for one performance with Ballet Theatre. In the early summer of 1974 she appeared at Covent Garden, breaking her stay in London for the first night of her production of *La Bayadère* for Ballet Theatre.

This was one of her most exciting experiences since she had come to the West, the first time she had ever mounted a ballet, and this in the face of considerable scepticism from American critics who doubted if the dancers of Ballet Theatre were really capable of the grand Imperial style demanded by this heroic work. Makarova was obliged to go back to the fundamentals of the classical dance, since the dancers all came from different schools and had no real understanding of classicism. As Makarova herself puts it, 'I had to go back to the beginning with them and teach them the basics of the classical school in which I was trained, and with each movement show them how to use their bodies to the fullest extent.' Each day she took videotapes of the rehearsals, studied them overnight and corrected faults the following day. Between herself and the girls of the *corps de ballet* grew a close relationship, based on affection and admiration, and this she greatly treasures. As well as uniformity of style, Makarova endeavoured to teach the dancers to achieve a flow of movement, both within the steps and also in the important linking passages, so that when the ballet came to be performed on 3rd July,

Rehearsing *Swan Lake* with Rudolf Nureyev and in *La Bayadère* with Mikhail Baryshnikov (American Ballet Theatre)

Antony Tudor's
*Romeo and Juliet*
with Paul Nickel

*La Fille mal gardée*
with Ivan Nagy
and (centre)
Enrique
Martinez
(American Ballet
Theatre)

1974, with Cynthia Gregory in the ballerina role, the public and critics were astonished by the classicism of the dancers, hitherto one of the main weaknesses of Ballet Theatre. Their views are typified by Arlene Croce who wrote in *The New Yorker*:

> She has not only reproduced a masterpiece of choreography, she has taken Ballet Theatre's *corps*—hardly the most sensitive choreographic instrument in the world—and recharged it from top to bottom. In place of the lifeless grey ensemble that had skated through *Giselle* and *Swan Lake* all these many years, there is now in *La Bayadère* an alert, disciplined and expressive *corps de ballet*, trembling with self-discovery.

In November of that year Makarova returned to the Royal Ballet where she danced for the first time the role of Manon. The dramatic range of MacMillan's choreography, the singular beauty and expressiveness of its four great *pas de deux* and the complexity of the character herself, have made this perhaps the most fulfilling role she has danced since leaving the Kirov. Here her gifts as a great dramatic ballerina were given full scope; all the moods—of guile, flirtatiousness, rapacity, and, beneath it all, an untouched simplicity—are woven into an expressive whole, rich in compassionate insight into this cruel but tormented being.

Yet few roles have caused Makarova such difficulties and self-doubt during rehearsal. I recall her telling me, almost in despair, how she could not grasp the nature of Manon, how she could not feel it. Then suddenly one day in rehearsal it all came right: she understood, gained an intuitive glimpse of the whole. Then she was at ease, despite a poor final rehearsal, and danced the role for the first time with a subtlety of musical thought and an understanding of character at a far deeper level than that attained by the fine dancers who had preceded her. It marked for her a new discovery in the classical dance, opening up wide perspectives, an undreamed of panorama of the future.

In April, 1975 she accepted the Royal Ballet's invitation to join them as a regular guest artist, and thus reached after five years of wandering her true artistic home. She appeared with them in their Big Top at Battersea Park, and despite the difficult conditions and shallow stage produced in *Giselle* one of her most astounding performances. An eminent choreographer who attended the performance told her it was the greatest piece of classical dancing he had ever seen in his life. Her partnership with Anthony Dowell had by now reached a stage of fine rapport; between them there was real understanding and imaginative sympathy.

After performances in *Swan Lake* and *Romeo and Juliet*, again in the 'Big Top', at the Newcastle Arts Festival, Makarova returned to London to appear with the Royal Ballet touring group in Ninette de Valois' *Checkmate*, an exciting experience both for her and de Valois, since they worked together with the closest understanding. Her admiration for Dame Ninette is boundless, and it is equally reciprocated. For the winter season at the Opera House, Makarova appeared for the first time in a ballet by Frederick Ashton, dancing the title role in *Cinderella*, and she was also seen in MacMillan's *Rituals* to music by Bartok and in Nijinska's *Les Biches*.

Makarova interrupted her London season in January, 1976 to dance with Ballet Theatre in New York in five performances, including *Giselle* and *La Sylphide*. Back in London, she danced in Balanchine's *Serenade* for the first time, rejoining Ballet Theatre for their tour of Los Angeles, San Francisco, Berkeley, Chicago and Washington. This was to be the pattern of the next eighteen months when she filled her double role as guest *prima ballerina* with the two companies—a unique position that she sustained with marvellous ease, making the necessary adjustments to two versions of the classics and a different company style with no discernible effort, while at the same time fulfilling engagements as a guest artist with the Miami Ballet, the Ballet do Rio de Janeiro in Brazil and a return visit to the PACT Ballet in South Africa.

On 19th April of this year she led the Royal Ballet at their opening performance of *Romeo and Juliet* at the Metropolitan Opera House in New York, achieving a great personal triumph. This was the first opportunity that her devoted New York public had to see her in this ballet and in *Manon*. After appearing with the Royal Ballet in Washington, she rejoined Ballet Theatre in Jerome Robbins' *Other Dances*, created for her and Mikhail Baryshnikov.

This gave her much delight, as she had always admired Robbins' choreography, recalling to me how she had been enchanted with *West Side Story* which she first saw in the Soviet Union. If she ever dreamed of appearing in his ballets, the idea seemed to her then so far-fetched and she too much of a realist ever to entertain it. This exquisite series of *pas de deux* means a great deal to her, since it fulfilled one of her main ambitions, not only in having a work composed for her but also dancing in a ballet by perhaps the finest of modern choreographers.

Makarova is like Anna Pavlova in that she does not worry particularly where she dances, either in great opera houses or in small theatres or in the Royal Ballet's tent, where she appeared in Plymouth in July and August, 1976. It must have seemed for her a long way from the Kirov Theatre to be next to a football ground in a large field, where the cheers from the fans mingled oddly with the anguish of Odette during one night's performance. When I met her after this, she said with a kind of bemused merriment: 'I don't know what on earth I'm doing here!'

In fact she much enjoyed the fun and sense of improvisation that the Company obtains from dancing in their tent, and they have great affection for her for this lack of pomposity and the professional courtesy that she shows towards them. It is this professionalism that has been remarked upon to me so often. I recall their astonishment on one occasion when, delayed by fog in Spain, she only arrived at Covent Garden half an hour before her performance in *Romeo and Juliet*. She had just time to complete her make-up in the wings, and, not having warmed up at all, gave a completely relaxed performance as if none of this had ever happened.

In October she was back in the United States dancing with Ballet Theatre in Washington, following this by a nationwide appearance on the Steve Lawrence and Eydie Gormé television show, where she performed the Can-Can to her evident delight. In November and December she was with the Royal Ballet at Covent Garden, appearing in Tetley's *Voluntaries*, where she alternated with Lynn Seymour in the leading role. At a gala she danced in the first performance of Hans van Manen's *Adagio Hammerklavier*. The new year saw her with Ballet Theatre in Mikhail Baryshnikov's new production of *The Nutcracker*, while in February, 1977 she appeared with the Scottish Ballet in Paris, dancing *La Sylphide*, partnered by Rudolf Nureyev, in the vast Palais des Sports. A further tour with Ballet Theatre to Los Angeles, San Francisco and Washington followed.

Perhaps the most exciting experience this year was to mount a single performance of Igor Tchernichov's *Romeo and Juliet* for the little Maryland Ballet. This was the ballet that had been created for her during her years at the Kirov and which had then been banned as too *avant-garde* by the Communist authorities. Makarova told the press that 'it was the only thing I regretted artistically when I left the Soviet Union, not having the opportunity to dance it'. Aided by Mikhail Baryshnikov, who had rehearsed the work with her at the Kirov, they were together able to reconstruct the choreography, and so rescue the ballet and recover a small part of their own past.

After a series of eleven performances with Ballet Theatre, including *The Firebird*, *Sleeping Beauty* and her own production of *La Bayadère*, Makarova returned to London to dance in *Swan Lake* with the Royal Ballet at Covent Garden in June. Then began her most demanding series of performances since she came to the West, dancing with Ballet Theatre in Vienna, returning to join Nureyev for three weeks of his season at the London Coliseum, followed immediately by a further week there with Ballet Theatre.

With Nureyev she danced *Giselle* on four consecutive nights, yet each performance was different in tone, the character seen in new perspectives—a truly extraordinary glimpse into the richness of her imagination. She also danced in Flemming Flindt's, *The Lesson*, a kind of surrealist nightmare, both funny and horrifying, as well as being at times slightly absurd. She appeared in a reconstructed Bournonville *pas de deux*, as well as in the *Corsaire* and *Don Quixote pas de deux*, in each case partnered by Nureyev. There were performances of *Les Sylphides* with Nureyev, Fonteyn and Lynn Seymour—surely the most remarkable casting since the ballet was first danced by Pavlova, Karsavina and Nijinsky in 1908. Even in so wretched a production, a small piece of ballet history was made.

After the London season, Makarova was in Paris with Ballet Theatre in the courtyard of the Louvre, where the opening night was badly curtailed by rain, so that she could not be seen in her production of *La Bayadère*. Immediately after this, she joined the Scottish Ballet in Edinburgh to appear in *La Sylphide* as part of the Festival. Even though she was very tired after so exhausting a summer, she danced the ballet with the same freshness that I had seen in Copenhagen two years earlier, setting the lithograph of her dancing exquisitely within the frame of its music. It brought to a close this hectic story of eighteen months, each performance a new adventure in her life and art.

# FIVE

# *The Inner World*

THE INNER WORLD of an artist's imagination is difficult to reach since it is guarded by words that express only inadequately the secrets hidden there. Although Natalia Makarova is highly intelligent and articulate (despite her somewhat irregular use of the English language) she works by means of her intuition as much as by logical analysis, so that it is impossible to discover at what point each of these faculties meet. A great deal, therefore, must remain unsaid, although it can be seen very clearly in her own dancing.

To discuss with her the meaning of the classical dance and the interpretation of its most celebrated roles is, however, to become aware of the high seriousness with which she approaches her art. For her the dance is not an outward show, it is an inner search—a discovery of truth and not an artifice of the theatre. I think that in her performances Balzac's maxim that 'the dance is a manner of being' achieves its widest relevance. Her dancing is not a concern for effect, however beautiful, but a means whereby the artificialities of the classical dance are employed to express a truth about human nature and human relations that will have a universal validity. She dances in terms of poetic metaphor, where the symbols of the classical technique and the imagery of its design are used in order to explore the hidden mysteries of the human heart. It is a voyage of discovery into an unknown land, apprehended intuitively, and expressed in the sublime logic of the classical style. Paul Valéry's

70

description of the poet as a combination of 'a cool scientist and a subtle dreamer' is an exact expression of Makarova's approach to her art, that is at once intuitive and, at the same time, coolly reasoned.

The classical dance is for her a kind of allegory for all the secret journeys of the heart. Each performance is a new exploration, a discovery of emotional truth of which she herself was not even aware. It is not a matter of mechanics or technique; it is a ceaseless quest for the meaning that lies beyond them, the shaping in plastic design of an imagined idea, accessible only through the creative imagination.

No one knows better than she the difficulty, even the impossibility, of such a quest. She has said to me that she is concerned only with the spiritual content of the dance, at the same time adding, rather wryly, that this is perhaps impossible to realise in terms of movement, when you have only a body and two legs to express it. No dancer of our time is more aware of the limitations of her art, nor so fiercely dedicated to extending them, and, by this, drawing closer to the frontiers of that visionary land where poetic truth is expressed in terms of metaphor. There can be no other true aim for the classical dancer, no other goal worthy of her inheritance.

The classical technique has never come easily to her, and it is surprising to learn this when one considers the fluidity of her dancing, as free as the rippling curve of a wave. On some days, she says, it 'just falls apart' in class or rehearsal where she finds herself struggling against a deep inner resistance to the purely mechanical nature of her task. She detests all that is mechanical and without feeling, since this denies the vividness of experience she seeks both in art and life. She can never, she says, dance the same step twice in exactly the same way, and I do not think we should take this literally, but rather in the sense that she cannot feel it emotionally second-hand. It must be new in the world of sensation, a new discovery in plastic design, and this is as true in the execution of a single step or pose as in the most complex dance or the most subtle exploration of character in terms of the dance.

Her body is exceptionally supple, and in many ways the classical style, demanding pure clear lines, a straight back and a high precision, runs counter, she thinks, to her natural means of expression. As she resists, so this conflict between her will and the technique of her art leads to an acute state of inner tension and frustration. It amazes her, this life of dedication to achieve the perfect movement: she says, 'Imagine it, for twenty-five years I have been attempting the perfect *pirouette* from the fourth position.' At these moments it appears to her an absurdity.

This profound distaste, even an inability, ever to do the same thing twice, thus affects her approach to the classical technique as much as it does to the interpretation of the role. Every time she dances, even in the routine of the classroom, she describes how she must sense for herself each movement as though it were being at that moment discovered, and there is a wonderful joy to her when suddenly and as if by accident it is perfectly achieved. Then she realises that it is perfect because this is the most simple means of performing it; the sense of conflict and resistance had been only in her inability to find the natural way. For this reason she considers the technique taught by Agrippina Vaganova the greatest yet evolved for the classical dance, since it is basically the most natural way of executing the steps.

On the stage she does not feel the same conflict between her instinct and the formal technique, for here it is harnessed to emotional expression and flows in a manner that is wholly organic, growing out of the music. It is then that she achieves a kind of inner freedom, where the movement is at one with the music and true to the emotion she feels. This harmony is not only observable from the audience, where the perfect balance and linear beauties of her dancing can be seen, but, more important, within herself when the conflict between her own nature and the technical means of expression is resolved in the flow of the dance. Makarova speaks much about this sense of inner freedom and release which in the dance we might equate to the resolution of harmonies in music.

At the same time she does not feel that the classical technique is a limitation upon her, nor that it impairs her powers of expression, and I think she finds the freedom claimed by certain modern dancers to be both superficial and too easily won. Indeed, the very constriction of the form allows her to seek for the greatest intensity of expression which might otherwise become diffuse or imprecise. As Makarova says herself, 'In every classical step you can bring something different. Any *arabesque* can sound different. You can put into it a whole variety of feeling.'

Makarova will maintain that she is not so devoted to the classical dance that she is content to remain solely bound by it, and she has little patience with those who speak of classicism with an excess of reverence. She is very serious about her art, but she is inclined to mock at solemnity, being temperamentally like a person much given to giggling in church. She admires iconoclasts, and is particularly enthusiastic about the work of Twyla Tharp, while her admiration for Jerome Robbins is in part due to his easy and unaffected attitude to the classical dance that is so apparent in his choreography.

What she asks above all from a choreographer is a freshness of vision, a series of new insights through which she can explore new aspects of her own personality. She does not want novelty for its own sake, but for her's: the potential is there, and her only frustration as a dancer is that much of it is still unexplored. It has been a disappointment to her that she has had no new role created for her, other than various *pas de deux*, during her seven years in the West, and it is exactly for this kind of creative excitement that she most hankers; in no other way, she feels, can she fully develop her art.

In rehearsal Makarova is concerned only with technical matters; details of interpretation are not worked out in advance, nor are they consciously planned. To watch her in rehearsal is to see no more than an outline sketch of the role, the bare bones of the choreography, and tiny details of the stage performance which she will when the time comes either discard or elaborate in an entirely different manner. It is like a painter's outline for the finished portrait which she roughs out, almost absent-mindedly, with her partner, her emotions at a deeper level entirely unengaged. It is as if she does not at this point wish to become emotionally involved either in the role or with her partner, since this will, she feels, impare the spontaneous creation of the role during performance.

Makarova has danced Giselle, her most famous part, on innumerable occasions, but, she tells me, it is never the same Giselle. As she waits behind the cottage door to make her entrance in the first act she is even then considering various different lines of interpretation: will the entry be care-free, doom-laden, impulsive or shy? At that point she is still unsure. Then she enters, and from then on the playing of the role is entirely different from any of the versions she planned in her mind. 'Quite different,' she says. 'But different better.'

I think this gives us a clue to the essential mystery of her art, that is at once so truly creative and so spontaneous. We do not watch a carefully rehearsed version of the role, where every detail has been meticulously filled in; rather we see a spontaneous creation, evolved moment by moment as a result of her personal identification with the music and her partner, and the mood in which she finds herself that particular night. I recall how, after an extraordinary performance in *Swan Lake* during the Royal Ballet season in Battersea Park in 1975, I remarked to her how surprised I had been at certain changes she had made in the presentation of the central role. 'I was surprised also,' she said. 'It just happened that way. I did not plan it so.'

In her dancing we see the role actually in the process of creation, the free play of her imagination around a set choreographic design. I remember watching a film of Picasso drawing on glass, presented in such a manner that one could see how each new thought or imaginative glimpse of the final design arose spontaneously during the act of creation. So it is with Makarova's performance in the great classic role—improvisations of her emotional and imaginative life, as she feels it at that particular moment, and which she will feel quite differently when she comes to dance the role again.

In every ballet she dances the role must be a personal insight rather than a conformity to any set libretto or a view of character given to her, as it were from outside. It is true, as she describes it, that this is not a matter of intellectual analysis but of feeling, to reach within herself for the source of the emotion she is to portray on the stage. Once she has discovered the truth of that feeling she will not change it, even at the suggestion of the choreographer, as long as that emotion is real to herself. For her the role is a unity and must be expressed harmoniously as a single vision into which certain ideas from others (though she can recognise their validity in intellectual terms) will not at that time be assimilated without damaging the total design. Possibly it was for this reason that her critics with the Kirov Ballet described her as stubborn, as she is, but only in the manner in which she guards the truth of her inner vision; if pressed too strongly she would, I feel, fight for it like a tigress for its cubs. In this sense it is not stubborness, but a fierce integrity, in life as in art, from which she will never deviate.

What Makarova fears before and during a performance is a certain deadness of feeling that allows her no scope. It is then that she is forced into a purely theatrical interpretation without any true spontaneity, either in her relationship to the music or to her partner, and these are the kinds of performance she chooses to forget. She agrees that for the audience a repetition of the same Giselle may be equally moving—indeed most ballerinas work in this manner; having established the kind of interpretation they wish to give, they do not alter it substantially in detail from performance to performance—but for herself it brings only despondency and a sense of creative loss. The governing factor, she insists, is her own emotional response; without this the dance is a dead and mechanical thing to her, of no value to her creative imagination.

The acid test by which she judges her own performances is that of sincerity. If there is no truth in the emotion she feels and projects, if, in fact, it is purely a matter of technique and theatrical skill, for her that performance is a failure, however enthusiastic may be the response from the audience and the critics. I have known her after a performance, at the end of which flowers rained down in a storm of applause, totally disconsolate. 'There was no truth in it,' she will say. 'I feel nothing truly.' This sense of failure isolates her, leaves her empty and dispirited, despite the cheering and the falling flowers.

The joys or griefs of her private life have little effect on her performance; either emotion is of use to her, as it gives her something upon which to work. But there must, as she waits in the wings or behind the cottage door in *Giselle*, be this spark of true feeling that she can then kindle into flame. Before she dances in *Giselle* she listens to music by Bach when she is resting at home, in order to give herself a sense of inner harmony and balance that she will find again in her dancing. A long period of anxiety, even fear, about her performance will be followed by a sense of vast lassitude and relaxation, and she finds this pattern of emotion the best prelude to the vividness of response she needs in the theatre. If all else fails during this period of preparation—music, the companionship of friends, or reading poetry—she will become desperate and go out and buy a shirt. 'I have hundreds,' she says. 'I needed them for *Giselle*.' Charming and unexpected as this is, one realises how essential it is for her to receive a kind of emotional lift, however small it might be, in order to dispel any sense of repetition or theatricalism in her dancing.

The long hours of deliberation before a performance that will keep her in a kind of private isolation are essential to her in order to achieve this sense of creative excitement upon which she must draw when she is dancing. Echoes of music, hints of her body's distant

harmonies, a curve in the air that will frame the dance entirely—
these fill her waking hours, disturb her when she should be sleeping.
No wonder she is impatient about the past; for the present entices
her, draws her, moth-like, towards the flame of her dancing.

Unlike many theatrical performers, Makarova seems to be quite
without envy; indeed I have only heard her speak ill of one ballerina.
For her Makarova shows nothing but dislike, and this seems to me
unfair as this dancer bore all the marks of a stupendous talent before
she was twenty-two years old. The dancer is, of course, herself—
Natalia Makarova, the dazzling young ballerina, whom London
first saw at Covent Garden in 1961. Maybe her young rival
challenges her still, even today, when she is without equal among
the ballerinas of both the East and the West. As we once went
through sets of photographs, I was astonished how censorious
Makarova became; for the nineteen-year old Natalia Makarova,
rising star of the Kirov, she had no good word to say. She was fat;
she had thick legs; her interpretations, caught by the camera, were
naive in the extreme. How, she wondered, could I ever have
admired this dancer so much when I first saw her dance, admired her
to such an extent when the other critics either ignored her, or treated
her as no more than another talented dancer in a company of
brilliant performers? It is inexplicable, Makarova implied, and
showed very dubious taste; what has happened since is entirely
irrelevant.

It is not, I think, that she disowns her past career; rather that it has
no immediacy for her any more. Her mind is fixed on the new role,
the one to be danced tomorrow; what came before, even what
happens afterwards, is of little consequence. It is the present she cares
about—these fleeting moments, so vital with life, so astonishing and
newly-made, containing within them the power to vivify her
imagination. She has, in fact, to imagine the role before she can
dance it, even if this dream of what it is to be is quite different from
the reality in performance. Her friends, and those whose taste she

77

values, are often of use to her. She will ring them up and say abruptly, 'How am I to dance Manon?' or 'How do you see my Giselle tonight?' The answers may be quite trivial, but they will be enough to give her something upon which her imagination can then work. It is a clue she needs, a starting point, just as a writer will seek for a single word that in itself will vivify his imagination. 'If each *Giselle* were not new for me, a new experience', she says 'I should never dance it again.' When I have discussed with her in isolation certain aspects of the interpretation of Giselle in her performance, she is inclined to get irritated: 'Which Giselle is that?' she will ask. 'I have hundreds of different Giselles.' It does not make life easy for a critic, but she certainly is not interested in *that*.

She knows, too, sometimes to an agonising degree, an artist's disquiet: what she achieves is never quite that for which she aimed, no interpretation contains all that she feels capable of giving. It is something, she says, locked inside her, and it has not yet been released; she is still frustrated by the potential she feels as yet unable to express.

I think that this continual quest for new meanings in familiar roles, such as Giselle or Odette-Odile, that brings to her dancing its astonishing resonances, the opening up of fresh perspectives in dance and characterisation, is to some extent to be found in her own attempt to create a harmonious balance in her own complex nature. I do not pretend to understand this: what human being ever understood another? But I am sure that her explorations in art cannot be separated from that perpetual inner struggle of a restless imagination, this quest always for intensity of experience.

It is for this intensity that she seeks continually, both in her art and her private emotional life. She is not temperamental, in the sense that Pavlova was, nor is her life a series of scenes and conflicts. As a person she is quiet, self-contained, in many ways self-deprecating, without small-mindedness or spite either in her professional or everyday life. She is in many ways quite the opposite to the boring picture of a great star; indeed some of her admirers are disappointed by her humility, just as her fellow artists admire her for exactly these qualities, and for the sense of vulnerability she carries within her. This contrast between extreme sensitivity and a fierce will, between a surface of wit and high-spirits and an inner melancholy, gives her enormous resources on which to draw as a performer.

The complexity of her nature, so rich and variegated, so finely poised between the intuitive and the rational, with all its shimmering lights and moments of darkness, is so closely mirrored in her dancing that it is impossible to separate the two. I wish to make this point early, and I shall return to it when I come to consider her dancing in all its richness and wide humanity.

It is the classical dance as a natural form of movement and as the expression of true emotion that is Makarova's final concern. She does not think of Giselle or Odette-Odile as imaginary persons, bound by a certain libretto, but in terms of herself and her own emotional life. 'I think of myself as a young girl in love,' she says. 'Not as Giselle. I try to experience the whole of that love, as I have known it, in my performances. It must be true to me. The libretto is not important.' For this reason her performances are never static, since her own inner emotional life is being developed and enriched by her own living, and it is from this she draws, as from the memories of what she has known in the past. There is one fixed point to which she continually returns: it must be sincere, and it must be true to herself. That is the meaning of the dance to her, the basis of her artistic belief.

If the character is a stranger to her in emotional terms, as, for example, that of Hagar, the frustrated, embittered spinster of Tudor's *Pillar of Fire*, she has to approach the role in terms of imaginative empathy. Her first two performances in the role with Ballet Theatre were not successful in her eyes, even though they

79

were highly praised. Then she went to the cinema and saw a film of Chekhov's story *The Lady with the Dog*, and in the performance of its central role she found the emotional truth she needed for Hagar. She tells me that afterwards when she danced the part she did not imagine herself to be Hagar, but the actress in the film who portrayed the lady with the dog; as a result, her performance gained enormously in conviction. It was more than empathy, rather a total self-identification with someone entirely unlike herself, that gave her an understanding of the role. The cinema has always had this power to stimulate her imagination, possibly because of her first marriage to a film producer with whom she often discussed technical matters relating to interpretation which have been of value ever since. They would, she tells me, spend hours discussing various aspects of Giselle and different means by which the character could be projected.

It is for these reasons that her relationship with her partner on stage is of primary importance, indeed the most important aspect of her performance. 'A *pas de deux*,' she told me once, 'is a dialogue between two people: there should be in it nothing artificial, since it is like life'. For her there is a true relationship, a kind of intuitive understanding of each other. Her partnership with Anthony Dowell of the Royal Ballet has been, she told me, a continual source of inspiration to her because of his acuteness of feeling and sensitivity of response.

Here again her sense of empathy is one of the governing factors in this partnership. She tries to visualise to herself how he would see her, and how he would react to her, seeing herself through his eyes. I remember her telling me of a recent performance in *Swan Lake* when, at the first meeting of Odette and Siegfried, instead of looking away from him in fear, as she had done on previous occasions, she looked full into his eyes; for a moment, she said, she felt within herself all the wonder of first love. He was taken by surprise, since they had rehearsed this first encounter differently, and immediately he responded. The emotional contact was then made, and from it

With Anthony Dowell in *Manon, Romeo and Juliet*
and (previous page) rehearsing *Giselle* (Royal Ballet)

the performance developed to a degree of intensity that amazed her. It is important, Makarova maintains, that this response must be achieved very early in the ballet, since it is more and more difficult to find as the ballet progresses. If this early response is made, the relationship on stage develops intuitively and is not consciously controlled by either dancer.

This relationship between herself and her partner Makarova describes as 'improvisations of feeling.' It is the central truth of her art, that which gives her the most profound creative joy. It is without any sort of artificiality, and exists within the formal theatrical world of the classical ballet below the surface of the dance and the shaping of its designs. To achieve it demands intense concentration, and the free movement of the imagination, unhindered by theories or consideration of the technicalities of the dance, for these have already been discussed with her partner during rehearsal in an entirely objective manner. Makarova has described to me her first performance in *Giselle* for Ballet Theatre with Mikhail Baryshnikov after his defection from the Kirov Ballet. During this performance she tried to disregard her own emotions entirely, and to devote herself to his own playing; to inspire him, and to reassure him. 'I forgot myself entirely,' she said; it was only his dancing that filled her imagination, so that she could draw from him an emotional response deep enough to carry him through so difficult a performance. The result still amazes her. 'It was,' she says, 'as if we were in a trance. We seemed in some way possessed, taken over by the dancing as if it had a life outside ourselves.' It happened only once; now she is content to dance with Baryshnikov, assured of his ability to carry a role alone, no longer in need of her support.

Great dancers must be egocentric; in Makarova's words 'they must love themselves' otherwise they will not make sufficient impact on their audience. I think, however, as this performance with Baryshnikov testifies, that she is unique in being able to set aside her own emotions for the sake of giving greater inspiration to her partner. In all her interpretations when, as she puts it, there is 'true communication' between them she is then able to reach the highest peaks of expressiveness.

She believes it is not only the most famous dramatic roles in classic ballet, such as Odette-Odile and Giselle, that still contain a world of meaning for her to discover, but works like *Casse-Noisette*, *Raymonda* and *The Sleeping Beauty* offer her great scope in the use of her creative imagination. They are also full of drama, high emotion and subtleties of characterisation, and in no way does she consider them purely in technical terms, or merely as studies in the linear beauties of the classical technique. Indeed she regrets that no producer seems yet to have grasped the subtleties and depth of truth contained in Hoffmann's vision of *Casse-Noisette* that has now degenerated into an empty, sentimental tale for children. She is far from believing that any of the great classical ballets are without emotional depth, and the more slender the theme the greater she feels is the challenge to her imagination. One never, she says, comes to the end of discoveries in any of the great roles.

If one asks her what she seeks in the classical ballet she will reply that 'I try for the most natural way of feeling, that is true in human life and not just on the stage.' To achieve this she must obtain a high degree of empathy with her partner, 'to know to which kind of humanity he will respond.'

Makarova will make no division between the dance and life, between her art and her living. For her the richest experience is when she feels most truly herself, devoid of all artifice or inhibitions—a sense of release in the full expression of her personality, which, she says, is the greatest delight of human communication whether in life or on the stage. To her the true aim of the classical dance is to realize what she describes as 'a visual, plastic ideal by means of feeling it through the body'. I think her genius as a dancer lies in the ability she has to find this human response within a formal style, where there is no divide between 'real' and 'stage' emotion.

It is difficult for her to describe how this communication is achieved, for she will deny that it depends upon analysis or conscious thought; it is, she says, what a woman feels within a growing relationship, a meeting of people at a deep, unconscious level. Here I am reminded of Rilke's beautiful remark when he describes love being the moment 'when two solitudes touch and greet one another'. Makarova who knows only too well the solitude of an artist will understand that, this response of a partner to a greeting in her eyes. 'You must speak with your eyes,' she says.

She has described to me how in earlier versions of her Odette-Odile she would, after she had changed in her dressing room in the interval between the second and third acts, deliberately cut from her thoughts all memories of Odette. 'I would look into the mirror,' she told me, 'and harden my eyes, make them cruel, without any pity or tears.' This change in her manner could not be achieved by artifice; it had to be created by a change in her inner emotional life, as if she took on, even became possessed by, this spirit of evil that was to destroy the Prince. She had to feel the evil inside her, in much the same manner as a novelist has to be 'taken over' by his character who then can speak with his voice and watch through his eyes.

Makarova's interpretation of the dual role of Odette-Odile in *Swan Lake* has undergone many transformations since she first danced it with the Kirov Ballet in 1959. At first it was sufficient for her to contrast the lyricism of Odette against the harsh and brilliant Odile, without seeking for great depths of characterisation in either role. Then she saw an old film of Ulanova and Plisetskaya in the part of Odette. Studying these two performances, as it were side by side, she was able to find a whole range of relationships and subtleties of interpretation contained in both versions of the role, so that she began then to make her own synthesis of these two different approaches. Between the divine simplicity of Ulanova and the highly-charged dramatics of Plisetskaya, she found her own centre, her own insight, that took something from them both but was for her in fact a new and personal creation. She considers that *Swan Lake* must be seen as an allegory of love, whereby instinctive nature can be transformed and sublimated by the power of love. Only the central relationship between Odette-Odile and the Prince matters, and it is here, she believes, that the profoundly symbolic nature of the ballet and its allegorical truth must be explored.

Makarova has discovered a new and more subtle meaning for Odile. Now she is highly critical both of her manner of playing the role in the past and of some present interpretations, where Odile is shown to be so obvious in her sensuality that no Prince would for a moment be deceived. Recently she sought to overcome this problem by presenting Odile as an evil spirit, indeed more like the spirit of evil itself, who hypnotises Siegfried until he is powerless to resist her. This is in line with C. W. Beaumont's suggestion in his book, *The Ballet Called Swan Lake*, that Odile is Von Rothbart's familiar spirit, rather than just his daughter as is stated in the scenario. Makarova told me how she imagined herself all evil, with the power to lay a curse on Siegfried which he would not be able to remove.

But now she sees Odile differently. 'There is bitterness in her,' Makarova says, 'the taste of bitter tears.' She sees Odile as a woman who has experienced much in life, known grief and spiritual suffering. When she meets the Prince she is aware that he has come too late into her life, and that such love can never be hers again. In contrast to Odette, a figure of immature love, she contrasts Odile as that same woman who has now known mature love in all its depth confronted as it were with young love again. Makarova describes her as 'a strong Odette'. She is, Makarova realises, forced to seduce Siegfried, but she will do it in her own way, and in doing so she will find real love awaken in her heart again.

In this interpretation Makarova plays down all that is flashy or evil in Odile, and stresses the similarities to the dancing of Odette that Petipa has made so evident in his choreography for this act. Her aim is to make the ballet a single vision of the nature of human love, as it is first experienced, and as it is known again in maturity. In a sense her Odile is Odette grown up. She is a character far more complex and subtle than the evil enchantress of the libretto; indeed Makarova considers her to be another aspect of femininity in contrast to the less mature Odette, and it is in the depths of her own nature that the ballerina must find her. Here again one sees how closely Makarova relates the artifices of the classical ballet to her own living. In the development and enrichment of her own character she finds new complexities and facets to the roles she plays on the stage, and these are in a continual state of transition as she herself learns and discovers more about her own nature.

No role, no interpretation of a role is with her a static thing. It is always an exploration, a search for truth. One can never say with her that she has now reached what one might describe as a definitive Odette-Odile or Giselle, for each night offers new discoveries in the dance and in the gradual transformation of the role. It may well be that her Odile will be different, vastly different even, from what I have described at this moment, for another year will have brought her new discoveries in her own nature that will find themselves expressed in the role. This is the great fascination of her art, both to herself and to her audiences—this sense of the adventures of the spirit in the quest for dramatic truth. This, Makarova stresses, will come out in the manner of playing both roles; it is a matter of style and emphasis, rather than any deliberate change in the scenario, or, of course, in the traditional choreography. She drew my attention to one small shift of emphasis at the end of the third act *pas de deux*: previously Odile took the Prince's hand with an almost brutal certainty; as Makarova puts it, 'she claimed him for her own'. In her most recent performances, she takes his hand gently, almost with trust, almost in love. These details, however little they may be noticed by most of the audience, are essential to her in obtaining the right emotional colouring for the dance. She must, here again, feel it in terms of human emotion, and relate to the real world, to her own understanding of human love.

Her approach to the role of Giselle shows the same sensitive response to human emotion, and her ability to see a part in its totality. Criticised by several people (including myself) for making the scene of madness too pathological in some recent performances, she felt she could not change it then, since Giselle, as she felt her within herself, could not react in any other way. 'When I feel Giselle differently,' she said, 'I shall be able to play the mad scene in a different way.' It is this grasp of the role as a single, developing unity of character that gives her performances in classical ballets their extraordinary vividness of perception and so rich a humanity.

For Makarova the only link between the first and second act of *Giselle* is the love she feels for Albrecht; all else is lost to her, all human feeling. She is immeasurably far from our world; she can, Makarova says, even smile, but she is too far away for more than the most remote pity. Yet her love for Albrecht remains, different maybe, and faint; it is the only sound from our world she is able to hear. In conversation Makarova put this point to me with great beauty. 'Nothing else can touch her but this sound,' she told me. 'It is all that is left with her in the grave.'

In the last analysis an artist works for his own sake, to fulfil an inner need. Makarova is fond of quoting Stravinsky's remark when asked for whom he wrote his music: 'For myself,' he replied, 'and one hypothetical other.' It is, she describes, rather like holding a conversation with oneself that is overheard by the audience. Of course she is influenced by their response, but during performances her concentration is so total that she is barely aware of them. Yet between herself and the music there is an almost physical relationship. 'I feel it in myself,' she says. 'It is as close to me as my own blood.'

As in her dancing there is no monotony of phrasing, despite the confines an unimaginative conductor may attempt to set around her, so at the same time there is a constant shift in emotional balance. In every ballet she dances we reach these points of the greatest expressiveness which I have described, but also discover the most subtle gradations of feeling within a single dance. Makarova has been criticised for the many changes of tempo she employs, but these are essential to allow her the widest range of emotional tone. If a ballerina does not phrase the music in this manner, Makarova considers she is ignoring the wider possibilities of the classical dance.

In my view western dancers are over-disciplined in this respect, so that they are not allowed a free play of the imagination, either within the music or the techniques of the dance. One can indeed maintain that Russian dancers, trained at the Bolshoi are too free with the classical form, and I would agree with this, but a balance can be achieved, as the dancers of the Kirov Ballet so wonderfully prove.

Obviously here the ideal is when the conductor and the ballerina work with one another in the closest collaboration in matters of tempo and phrasing, but this is not easily attained because of the limited time available and also the few rehearsals with orchestra that are economically possible for any ballet company. Makarova gave me an interesting example of this ideal state when she danced in Philadelphia in a performance of *Les Sylphides*. She was surprised during a final rehearsal with piano that the conductor was present and watched every detail of her performance. When she asked him about this, he replied that he was studying her in order to achieve the right phrasing from the orchestra to match her own. The result, in performance, delighted her to a greater extent than she had ever known before. 'It was,' she says, 'just like one. Not as if I danced with the music, or the music with me, or I am all music: it was all of these things together.' This seems to me a perfect summary of the relationship between the dancer and the music, which I have left exactly in her own words.

Makarova is fully aware of the difficulties in achieving the greatest plasticity of movement within the limits of the classical style. For her the dance is a conflict between emotion, which is free and unconfined, and the discipline of the form through which this emotion must be shown; this difficulty being expressed in music by the conflicting demands of phrasing and tempo. Indeed it is in the resolution of these central conflicts in the mysterious harmonies of her art that her genius as a performer resides. She and I are at one in this, for, above all, I seek for the unbroken flow of the singing line, rather than the clipped, staccato effect of the dancer who cuts up the music into thin slices like a stick of salami.

As her dancing contains aspects that are both intellectual and intuitive, I asked her if she could distinguish between intuition and imagination in her approach to her role. This is a question about which she has thought deeply, and her views cannot be given better than in her own words, which I have edited only by cutting out repetitions and changing the grammar slightly because of her imperfect knowledge of English.

You can describe intuition (Makarova says) as the part that comes first when you are considering a role. When this does not help further, you extend the first insight by means of the imagination. Roles to which you are born, which are in your blood, do not need imagination, but in a role like the Black Queen in *Checkmate* or Odile, which are not in my nature, I have to use my imagination. My early Odile had not been developed so; it took several years to deepen the picture. I was not, when I first danced the role, prepared either as a dancer or as a person to grasp the nature of such a complex human being, as I had not the experience of life. I have to find a balance that will work in accordance with my kind of nature, yet, at the same time, will be an interesting interpretation for the audience. All my imagination, all my education, all my knowledge of life are in the role.

Intuition Makarova defines as natural knowledge, while imagination is creative knowledge. In rehearsal or on the stage she will

suddenly achieve a moment's insight into the nature of the role—
the character, the style, the quality of movement. At the same
time she holds in her mind an aural/visual picture of it, in the form
of a plastic design, towards which she moves as rehearsals develop.
'The role must become a part of my second nature before I can
express it,' she says, and this process may take a considerable time,
far longer, in fact, than that required to learn the choreography.

Makarova trusts her intuition entirely, but not her imagination.
Here the glimpses either technical or emotional into the role which
she discovers during rehearsal are later lost and have to be re-
discovered. It is an abiding fear that she will lose them forever. It is
for this reason that each performance in a classic role, such as Giselle
which she has danced on innumerable occasions, must be freshly
imagined and different in interpretation from one performance to
another. What she values most is what she describes as 'those sudden
moments of insight in which I feel sure of the nature of the role. It is
then you look into the centre of your imagination and not around it.'

If one asks Natalia Makarova what is the greatest joy she finds in
her art, she will reply that it is the struggle with her body to bring it
into conformity with her will:

> I like to fight with my body, and achieve a victory over it. When
> you are working on some technical problem, even at the point
> when you despair of ever solving it, then it suddenly resolves
> itself. You feel so happy, so amazed because it is now seen to be
> so simple. You feel light, at ease with yourself. It is only a
> wonder why you did not see something so easy before. This is
> one of the dancer's greatest moments, even if, suddenly, it is lost
> again. This is art, and this is life: there is no difference.

She believes that to retain what you feel at these moments, either
technically or emotionally, is the most difficult task of all. With
experience she now finds it easier as it were to hoard up these
moments of insight and to recover them in performance, but always
there is the fear they will be lost and will never be gained again. It is

for this reason, she says, she feels always so insecure: nothing is finally won, no imagination will run forever true.

It is the most cruel irony of a ballerina's life that her technique begins to decline even as she is in sight of her goal. At last she has achieved sufficient insight, a full grasp of her art, only to find that she is unable any longer to give it complete expression. It is this sad truth all dancers face towards the end of their careers, disguise it how they may by cutting out difficult steps or performing simpler roles, but it is one Makarova, as all the great dancers before her, has faced with a kind of defiance that mocks at time and all its cruel ambiguities. She explained this to me with great simplicity and beauty:

> There will be a kind of emptiness when it is finished, when I shall not be able to explore my body any more and let it speak to me.

Happily that time is still far in the future: the moment is now, this and the following years, now while her genius flowers in all its distant beauty.

I think what most strikes me about Natalia Makarova is the prodigality of her imaginative life, the hidden resources from which she is able to draw. To this must be added an almost child-like apprehension of the moment, to be caught, in the dance as in life, swiftly and with a sudden daring. Her concern that each experience should be a new one, a new insight, gives to her art this extraordinary sense of improvisation. I have tried, as far as I have been able, in conversation with her to discover the inner working of her imagination but it is not easily grasped in words. It is best known in music, in poetry and in her dancing. If art were no longer a mystery, it would no longer be relevant to us, and I know when I watch her dance that the secret remains, hidden behind her watchful eyes. A great poet, W. B. Yeats, perhaps best describes her:

> . . . and though some said she played
> I said that she had danced heart's truth.

# SIX

# *The Outer World*

## MAJOR ROLES

THERE IS at the centre of the classical dance a strange duality. For it is both an artifice and an aspect of nature, an art of extreme elaboration in form that is truly human in content. The impersonality of its structure allows the humanity of the dancer and her role to speak from within it in a manner that is unique in theatrical art. Form and content in ballet are divisible, yet they speak to us together; we see them as different aspects of the same truth. The abstractions with which it deals are shaped by the human body—not by words or notes of music, not by paint on canvas—so that the material is rich with its own life in a way that words or music can never be. Further, the dancer is her own instrument: she is the singer as she is the song. We can thus never divorce this most abstract of arts from the humanity that lies at its heart.

Indeed it is this contrast between the warmth of vital life, possessed by the dancer to a much greater extent than any other theatrical performer, and the impersonal nature of the classical technique through which she reaches us, that the eternal fascination of the art resides. The ballerina is like us, mortal and imperfect, yet she speaks in a language that is both timeless and universal, refined in its beauty, cold in some ways, distant even as the moon. We are near her as she dances, for her movements, however stylised, are our own; yet she is far from us also—a small, isolated figure, assaulted by light and music, on a remote stage—one who inhabits an imaginary world like that of our dreams. She is a young woman yet she is an immortal spirit, and she is each at the same time.

The classical dance has tamed and formalised the most basic of all human means of expression, but it has not in the process weakened it or quenched those primitive fires. If we were able to free our emotional life, it would express itself in movement in the same manner a child does as he stamps or jumps or spins around in excitement, echoing the first dances of mankind in the instinctive dark. A *pas de deux* is, on this level, at one with the mating rites of animals or primitive man, while each gesture the dancer makes, codified as it has been down the years, is one of our own unconscious gestures that has, as it were, been brought under control and deliberately willed. The dance can, in fact, be seen as bringing the will in control of our unconscious life; it is the willed, as opposed to the instinctive act.

Beyond this the dancer is an expression of the unity in nature, the dance of all created things. They are contained in her dancing if she chooses to invoke them. She is sole guardian of the magical isles, for she can shape with her arms the curve of the wave, the flight of the autumn leaves; the moon can be called up at her bidding, or a constellation of stars. She has a world of slumbering images within her limbs; compact of all beautiful movement, the dance is stretched out before her like an enchanted landscape. She has the power to make the trees unfold, the flowers awaken, even, if she chooses, in the magnanimity of her art, to allow the snow to let fall its astounding blossoms, or shape the passing of the unseen wind.

We should not try to diminish the power of the classical ballet to speak to our emotions or its unique ability to join all nature together in one creative act. A dancer when she takes the stage contains so much within her small frame: she is a girl, the crest of a wave, the joyous leaping of our spirit, an image of our unconscious life, an imaginary character, a fragment of a vast design, a study in pure form. The old classical ballets survive for this reason: Aurora, the dawn, is all our mornings, our youth and the awakening of our heart. She is the Spring and the return of Spring. She is a design of sublime proportions. Similarly Carabosse is our own winter, our ageing and our disappointed love: she is the darkness that comes at the end of the long bright day.

Natalia Makarova is the inheritor of this great tradition, a style of dancing which is (in Levinson's words) 'one of the most stupendous discoveries in theatrical art'. She is aware of this, conscious of her inheritance and of her responsibilities towards the art and the future of that art. She is perfectly schooled in the Imperial style of the Russian Ballet, which has been enriched in expressiveness by the discoveries in movement of Agrippina Vaganova, while her creative imagination is such that she has the potential to extend its range far beyond the boundaries set by her great predecessors. In a sense she summarises what has gone before, contains it in her dancing, and in doing so points the way to the unknown future.

If, as we have seen, the inner world of an artist's imagination is the centre of her creative life, there is always the outer world to which this life is exposed. The difficulty of criticism is that one must relate the two, seeing one as the expression of the other, and with a ballerina as deeply committed to the emotional truth of the roles she portrays, we must see these both objectively as theatrical events and subjectively as the expression of her own nature. We must look both at her dancing and beyond it.

All art is indivisible; in whatever medium an artist works he will relate to other arts, however diverse are the means they employ. Closest of all to the dancer is the poet, and I know no more exact description of Natalia Makarova's dancing, for example, in the great *pas de deux* in the second act of *Swan Lake* than these words of Keats in one of his letters:

> The rise, the progress, the setting of Imagery should, like the sun, come natural to him, shine over him, and set soberly, although in magnificence, leaving him in the luxury of twilight.

Here is contained the sense of space, the wide proportions and the concept of the dance as a single design, that is central to her art, where a variation or a *pas de deux* is seen whole and not as a series of isolated fragments. You cannot take Makarova's dancing to pieces: it is a unity, where each section grows organically from that which precedes it, bound together by a single sweep of the imagination, leaving us at its conclusion 'in the luxury of twilight'.

During the years before I first saw Makarova dance I had been gaining an insight into the type of classical dancing I held as an ideal, even though no ballerina, however eminent, had been able to express it for me in its entirety. There had been hints, no more than that; moments of understanding when I glimpsed what the classical dance could mean. It is this, I would think, but it is more than this; perhaps in fact it can never be achieved, and those who wrote of Anna Pavlova and Olga Spessivtzeva were, in fact, deceived.

It is true, of course, that I saw great ballerinas, all of whom brought something different to the dance. I remember Alicia Markova who could alight on a musical phrase with a kind of airy precision, like a dragonfly settling on a shimmer of luminous wings. Her style was so fastidious, a sort of delicate embroidery with the threads of the music, swift and full of bright, glittering movements, so that her dancing seemed to glance at you side-long, evasive and mysterious like a fleeting smile. Dancing in the same wonderful seasons of the newly-formed Festival Ballet was Yvette Chauviré, whose performances had a type of icy distinction, full of marbled phrases like the poetry of Racine, in which each statement of the dance was made with a kind of finality as if a life depended on it.

Impersonal, gravely eloquent, it was like a piece of sculpture carved out of the music in the slow unfolding of each formal step, heroic in its proportions, so harmonious in its moments of repose. In some way it brought the classical dance close to its roots in the Court ballets of France in the seventeenth century; one saw it, like a statue or a fountain at Versailles, in the long perspective of the music as though glimpsed through an avenue of trees. So many dancers of the English school seemed cramped in comparison, as if they were forced to crowd their movements within the music where they had not space to expand and flower.

I developed a great admiration for the dancers of the modern French school—for Jeanmaire, so witty and sensual, making the dance into a kind of epigram, neat and perfectly formed like the maxims of La Rochefoucauld; for Vyroubova with her magical arms that seemed to float on the music like shadows over moving water; for Skorik with her enigmatic smile, half Gioconda, half *demi-mondaine*. Above all, like the majority of my generation, I retained as my guiding star the dancing of Margot Fonteyn.

It has been lost now, the extraordinary poetry of her dancing, so pure, so mysterious, so full of distant echoes; it reminded one of the songs from Shakespeare's plays, the verse of Herrick, Campion and John Clare. It was both artless and highly sophisticated, with a clear, singing line I have found again in no other ballerina, full of a curious sense of nostalgia for a world of ideal beauty whose reflection lingered in her wondering eyes. I never expected to see a dancer as great as her again.

When the Bolshoi Ballet arrived in London in 1956, headed by Galina Ulanova, the excitement was enormous, the drama splendidly enhanced by threats of cancellation owing to the arrest of a Russian lady who had stolen some hats. Here, we thought, is the real thing, the Russian ballet at last. For many, whose judgement I respect, the dancing of Ulanova was a revelation; for me, it was wonderful in its sweep, in the flow of movement, the sense of total sincerity. None the less it did not fulfil my ideal. Indeed I thought, like all ideals, I should never find it. But I was wrong.

Natalia Makarova danced the role of Giselle for the first time with the Kirov Ballet at Covent Garden in 1961. It took me about ten minutes to recognise that she was a potential genius, rather too long by the standards of Sir Harold Hobson, who, writing in the *Sunday Times* some years later about the ballerina, affirmed that he could recognise genius, as he saw it in her, in—if I remember—about ten seconds flat!

Makarova's genius is that she makes all things new. She gives to old ballets new life, sets them in an entirely different perspective by the power of her creative imagination. The choreography of a familiar ballet like *Swan Lake* is magically transformed, so that it becomes a search for the meaning of mortal love. It is a new creation, built on a familiar theme, in the same manner as Beethoven took a banal little tune of Diabelli, and made from it those sublime variations, tremendous in their insight and their troubled dreams. When she dances, it is as if she created the ballet from that instant, each step freshly minted, seen anew, now full of strange resonances, the opening of sudden perspectives in thought and imagination. We are told this story of the enchanted Princess by the lakeside as if for the first time: the old tale has become strange to us again, full of mystery, glimpses of a dark truth. The primal myth of the struggle between light and darkness comes alive; it is elemental, a story told to us in the dawn of the world. The myth takes on once more its true validity within our unconscious life, and speaks in images as articulate as the language of our dreams.

I think what first astounded me when I saw Makarova dance was the manner in which she could create a new style of movement appropriate to each different ballet. It is not just a matter of emotional tone, but also the quality of movement. In *Swan Lake*, even

*Cinderella* with Anthony Dowell (Royal Ballet)

*Don Quixote pas de deux* with Donald MacLeary and *Les Sylphides* with Anthony Dowell (Royal Ballet)

as far back as 1961, her dancing was huge in scope, so that the *pas de deux* of the second act became a study in shifting lines, monumental in their proportions. It was a piece of living architecture, grand as a castle set on a hill, noble in its sweep of imagery, the huge logic of the total design. In Sergeyev's *Cinderella* the dancing was sharp, brilliant, daring in its phrasing, with a kind of glancing wit and a fragile elegance that reminded me of Alicia Markova. It was a world away in feeling from her Odette, more sophisticated than anything one could have expected. In *Giselle*, then as now, there was the amazing contrast between the warmth of her dancing in the first act and its spirituality in the second; both acts seen in terms of lithograph, but without being stylised in the manner of her performance in *La Sylphide* which is painted in a far lighter emotional tone, more a sketch, airy and delicate, than a portrait drawn in depth. I once displeased her by describing her dancing as Mozartian, since she felt she was unworthy of such a comparison, but I shall have to take the risk again. The range and the huge variety of styles she is able to discover in different roles makes such a comparison inevitable. She is not one dancer, but many: the universality of her art is prodigious in its variety like a source of nature. I am not afraid of such comparisons.

We have seen in the previous chapter how the ballerina's search for imaginative truth in each role she dances gives us this sense of a new creation. In terms of technique it is achieved by the varying of stress, dynamics and rhythm within the musical phrase, so that those images in the dance that have the greatest expressive power are most strongly projected. From the first moment I saw her I was struck by the clarity of each step, the manner in which it was shaped with an unhurried calm, growing organically out of that which preceded it, creating its own rhythm in the ebb and flow of the dance that was as free as the movements of nature—the rippling of the wind, or the beating of waves on the shore. In her dancing there is this continual contrast between strong and less strong images, where the emotional impact varies like that in the stanzas of a poem, and these relate in parallel to the musical line.

At all costs Makarova seeks to avoid any sort of rhythmic monotony in the dance, and few things disturb her more than a conductor who will allow her no variants in the shaping of the musical line. For her, true musicality is found in this visible shaping of the phrase, what one might call 'the breathing of the dance' where each of these phrases is then formed into wider paragraphs, proportioned in their relationship to the whole. It is an extreme elaboration of the classical form, architectural in its structure, where the phrase is like another arch, another pillar balancing the whole design.

As Serge Lifar has pointed out, the musicality of a dancer is seen in her movements, as well as in her relation to the music itself. Movement itself has become musicalized. In its proportion, the shaping of the visual line, the balance of accents in the rhythmic flow of the dance, are seen a kind of visual music. Makarova's dancing is orchestrated, richly composed as a symphony, when each line is set in a true relationship with the others, as themes in music balance and harmonize.

Makarova finds her own freedom in the classical dance, not by distorting it or bending its rules, since each step is executed with its full academic precision, but by giving the greatest plasticity to the flow of images. Each step is carried through the whole body into the next, so that we get the impression of images forming and fading one into the other in a way that is almost cinematic. Yet hold one single frame, as it were, and it will be proportioned exactly in accordance with the academic style. Here dancers often cheat; they blur the steps, sometimes by leaving them half formed, sometimes by omitting a detail, or eliding one passage into the next, in order to achieve this sense of flow. It is better, I agree, than the staccato dancer, where each phrase is cut off before the next begins to form, so that one has a kind of stammer in movement which often looks spectacular but is in fact a crude distortion of the classical style. The one may be a cheat, but she can produce a pleasing effect if you do not look too closely; but the other is an aberration. Makarova never cheats in technique: she is too well schooled by the Kirov to do that, while temperamentally it would be a dishonesty in art, and of that she is quite incapable.

If one considers her dancing in the balcony scene of MacMillan's *Romeo and Juliet* or in the last act *pas de deux* in his *Manon* one can see how great is the freedom she is able to gain within the classical style. This is partly achieved by *plastique*, to which I have already referred, but also by a kind of emotional intensity that sweeps the dance forwards, almost it seems, unwilled. Here Makarova dances like one possessed, caught up within the music and the intensity of her own emotion, so that the dance is apprehended by her (and so by her audience) on an instinctive level. It can be analysed technically; filmed in slow motion it would be academically flawless, but it goes beyond technique into the realm of pure emotion. In *Romeo and Juliet* the music and the poetry meet in her dancing, and in it they are reconciled.

The *pas de deux* in the last scene of *Manon* produces exactly the opposite effect but at the same level of intensity. Here there is no passion left, no ecstasy; only the last sighs of the exhausted spirit, purged of all feeling, a ghost who lives on reluctantly in a body already dead to this world. It is an extraordinary achievement in choreography to be able in two different ballets to reach the two most distant poles of human experience—an intensity of sensual awareness at the one extreme, the exhaustion of all feeling at the other—and I think Kenneth MacMillan has not received the recognition that is his due for such imaginative insight and under-standing of the emotional life. He is fortunate, also, in having found a ballerina who is able to follow him to such distant lands and to reveal his choreography with such truth.

In this last scene Makarova dances as one beyond grief, beyond love; she lives in a night of dead stars. Anguished, she leaps into her lover's arms for the last time, and all her exhausted spirit clings to him, to die on a final kiss. Her dancing flickers like a dying flame; it burns brightest even at the moment when it fades.

A unique feature of Makarova's dramatic playing lies in her intuitive understanding of the role as an organic unity, rather than as a succession of emotional stages in the development of character. What has passed remains, even if it is only glimpsed at moments: so in *Manon* the child lives on in the woman in love, the innocence is not wholly lost even when it has been degraded; the love is there, hidden in the dream world of childhood, marvellously evoked in the choreographer's vision of the soft eddies of the music at Manon's entrance in the first act that are as gentle as the fluttering of her heart. In this scene Manon is barely awakened, yet as she touches her throat when she observes a woman's jewelled necklace one gets the first glimpse of the courtesan she is to become. Here the music entices her, draws her towards its flame, only then to return to the secret dreams of a child. Similarly, when she has completed the superb duet in the second scene, the child is now transfigured into the woman in love; left alone, she dances a group of tiny, skipping phrases, and the child has for a moment returned, one who bounces back into bed with an enchanting abandon as she must have done those lost years ago.

In the brothel scene the sophistication is only a veneer: beneath it is melancholy, boredom and certain sad remembrances that in reverie she conjures up, marking the passage of her thoughts by the tapping of her fan. This she will hold with a kind of posed coquetry across her cheek as this lost child mimics the woman of the world. Even her solo in this scene is not truly sensual or abandoned; it is gravely done, a lesson she is slow to learn. One is struck by the total self-absorption—in her hands, her jewels, the set of her dress, but one feels she is so self-regarding because she feels unloved and so much alone.

As the child lives on in the woman in love, so here the terrible loneliness of the last scene is prefigured; at every moment in her playing she leads us back into the past even as she draws us into the future. The whole narrative is thus encapsulated, where each isolated scene is lit by the past even as that light throws shadows into the future. This is the truth of Makarova's art, poised between past and future, both as living memory and distant foreboding, as it is the truth of life also, for we never escape our past selves even as our present carries its intimations of what is to be. In her dancing past and future are enclosed in a single vision, that is the wonder of her art.

This extraordinary gift to see a character as a unity is also one of the most remarkable features of her now legendary Giselle. From the outset we are confronted by a girl whose mind is, even within the excitement of first love, darkened by a terrible sense of foreboding. She does not know from where it comes or what is the reason, but it is hinted at in her frightened eyes, the nervous glances, the swift changes of mood that chase one another like the shadows of that autumn day.

She is a girl who grasps at a hope in which she does not believe, a pledge that even as she gives it she knows will be betrayed. At first she is like a small wild creature that has crept into the light, vulnerable and alone, trusting so much and so little, and so afraid. She is disturbed by each faint tremor in the music that is like a shiver of recognition, the knowledge sought for in an unspoken question, a game with flowers. It is a dream of love that has enchanted her, and it is only the truth she cannot face that would keep her sane. One can see it in the way she will not at first meet Albrecht's eyes. It is in part modesty, for she does not wish him to see the love she cannot hide; but it is also fear that she might discern the first hint of betrayal in his own.

The famous test with the flower petals in the first act here takes on an almost unbearable poignancy as for a moment she freezes in a sudden constriction of fear, her hands twisting the stems of the now prophetic flowers. We are made aware of the tenuous grasp she has on life and reason, how little it would take to drive her mad. Always in Makarova's interpretation one is conscious both of the intellectual concern for the logic of character and the intuitive workings of her imagination from moment to moment in the ballet. Between these two aspects, both of her art and of her own personality, the most delicate balance is achieved; indeed it is the central feature of her art, the one that places her alone among her contemporaries.

It seems to me, in fact, that the unique quality of her dancing is achieved by this most subtle balance between will and insight, between intellectual grasp and intuitive perception. It is this that gives it meaning far beyond the roles she plays on the stage; it is closer to her own life, and so to our own, embracing each in a single vision. Like the dancing of Anna Pavlova, her art is an expression of her nature, a sharing with us of her own humanity—even its perplexities, its inner doubts, its continual struggle to make a harmonious balance between conflicting demands. When I watch Natalia Makarova dance I am often reminded of Keats' words concerning 'the holiness of the heart's affections and the truths of the imagination'.

In the second act she moves, distant and luminous in the hazy light of the music, like the glimmer of the hidden moon, a troubled dream to haunt Albrecht's imagination in the darkness of his grieving. He grasps at this shadow, impalpable as air or the night winds on which she is floating. She achieves the perfect reconciliation where the spirit of the dead Giselle is still an echo of the betrayed girl. As she rises from the tomb she brings with her the chill of the abandoned grave, the darkness of the cold earth. There is in her dancing a terrible sense of mortality, the loneliness of the soul in the huge void between two worlds. In her performance it is not the dance itself but, as it were, the dance reflected in the still waters of the music, where it shimmers in the light, glows in its own iridescence. It is the dance made so impalpable that it is like a distant reflection of the dancer.

Nothing showed more clearly the huge interpretative range she can bring to a single role than performances in *Giselle*, danced first with Rudolf Nureyev and then with Mikhail Baryshnikov at the London Coliseum in the summer of 1977, more than two years after her last appearance in the ballet in London. These indicated not only her powers to adapt to her partner, but also her ability to present a classic ballet from two entirely dissimilar angles, each throughout consistent in tone.

I would like to consider these performances in some detail, since they indicate how her dancing continues to develop and how new insights have been discovered in a role which she has danced so often yet is still as fresh to her as if she were to dance it for the first time tomorrow.

Although Nureyev partnered her with great consideration and technical skill, there never seemed to be the close rapport between the dancers that is essential to her if she is to achieve the free improvision of feeling, as she describes it, that makes her dancing of the classics so ardent, spontaneous and far-ranging. Further, they were dancing in the Festival Ballet production with which they were both unfamiliar, containing Mary Skeaping's brilliant reconstructions of the original Perrot choreography and new dances that are a superb pastiche of nineteenth century ballet, and neither seemed entirely at ease.

As a result, Makarova aimed for the utmost simplicity and emotional intensity, where the dramatic lines of the first act should be drawn with strength and clarity, rather than in the accumulation of subtle detail that one can observe in performances where she has a closer emotional rapport with her partner. The style was flawless, pure Kirov, set in sublime proportions, so that the dance at its close faded away into the music with a wonderful finality. When she

completed a variation in the second act, the climax was like a
diminishing sigh, as if her limbs dissolved on the night air; one
recalled Gautier's beautiful description of Giselle as 'a cloud on two
legs'.

These 'dying falls' at the end of her solos have in these latest
performances become one of the most exquisite features of her art;
the final pose expands and fades, exactly as in music when the last
chord opens and falls away into silence, so that the stage is haunted
by the movements with which she closes her dances; they are like
a series of echoes in a luminous quiet, the silence after ended song.

In a new approach to the scene of madness, Makarova sought for
bold, harshly drawn images, as if it were seen through a tragic,
distorting imagination, one that belonged particularly to the
writers of the late nineteenth century. It is therefore later in time
than the period of the ballet, as it is enshrined in lithographs,
belonging more to the almost decadent age of romanticism,
described in Mario Praz's great book, *The Romantic Agony*.

Makarova is deeply interested in painting, and in this portrayal of
madness I think she may have been influenced by the surrealists
whom she much admires and the reproductions of whose painting
she has shown me in the past, speaking with such excitement as she
pointed out details in the work.

The lines were harsh and jagged, the movements seen between
flashes of lightening, lit with the same icy brilliance, the poses set
within a kind of monumental stillness, grief sculptured in a second
of frozen desolation, so heavy as if she were never to move again.
One thought of Yeats' famous poem: truly in this enactment 'a
terrible beauty was born'.

Makarova's single performance with Baryshnikov and the
American Ballet Theatre was quite different from this, the romanticism set exactly in period, so that we encountered the world of
Perrot and Coralli seen in terms of lithograph and soft line. The
difference between this performance and those danced with

Nureyev could not have been more striking. The sense of rapport was so close that they played to one another with a kind of spontaneity marked by the free use of a shared imagination.

Because Baryshnikov is so young a dancer, so ardent in expression and vibrant in feeling, Makarova responded to this by the most youthful and fresh Giselle I have ever seen her perform. So fragile at her first entry, she established at once all the pathos and the sweet vulnerability of the very young. It would take so little to destroy her, even as an early flower would wilt in the first frost, shrivel away in the cold winds of spring.

Makarova's dancing was of the purest kind, sketched in soft lines against the music, blurred and translucent, as if the music threw a nimbus of light round her limbs. It had the extraordinary effect I have mentioned earlier of seeming to fade away into the music, while the gradations between strong and gentle movements, the grandeur of spacing the musical phrases, the continual changing of dynamics within a single dance, gave these solos a fitful quality so evocative of spring.

This was Giselle seen not in terms of Petipa but of Perrot, and one wonders whether her experience of dancing in a Bournonville *pas de deux* earlier in this season had set her imagination thinking in terms of the more rounded movements that were so much a part of the Franco/Danish school of the dance. Her arms were set in more ample, softer curves, the line more gentle, even at times hesitant, as if she barely trusted her movements to the air—a perfect expression of the character of this particular Giselle, so tremulous with happiness, so fearful that she may lose this happiness for ever.

Makarova had recovered the feeling of her first Giselle in 1961 that so haunted my imagination ever since, though now it was surrounded by a technical virtuosity and a sense of dramatic nuance unknown to that young dancer: one felt she responded to her young partner by recalling her own Giselle from the past; she made it her gift to him, recognising as she does how much his own dancing summarizes the continuity of the great tradition in which she was schooled.

I was struck again by the beautiful magnanimity of her art and her character of which it is an expression, how she seeks always to find an accord with her partner, to share his world rather than impose her own vision upon him. It is a measure of her humility, as it is of her greatness.

The freshness of this performance brings to mind the poetry written in the early part of the nineteenth century; in particular I recall a poem of John Clare's written almost exactly at the time *Giselle* was composed: it summarizes so much about Makarova's dancing that I have tried to convey, but so simply, so directly, like her own art:

> And where is voice
> So young, so beautifully sweet
> As nature's choice,
> When spring and lovers meet?
>
> Love lies beyond
> The tomb, the earth, the flowers, and dew.
> I love the fond,
> The faithful, young, and true.

These two stanzas encapsulate for me perfectly what was contained in this performance, take one to the heart of this Giselle, 'the faithful, young, and true'.

Retaining the romantic spirit of the ballet, Makarova played the mad scene in a manner entirely in accord with it. This was the 'douce folie' critics had noticed in the performance of Olga Spessivtzeva, a madness seen wholly in terms of the romantic imagination, not surrealistic as in her performances with Nureyev, but lyrical and pathetic, the harsh lines softened, the anguish muted to a broken sigh. One moment she retained, and it struck one forcefully because of the gentler background: as she circles the stage, she tries to push some encroaching evil away from her with both arms; one knows that at that moment she is surrounded by demons, perhaps even that she sees the evil Myrtha and the dance in the dark wood for the first time, and tries to thrust it away from her. It is a moment of terror, perfectly placed within a setting of pathos, like a sudden discord that tears the heart.

A feature of her playing, much developed from previous performances, was the manner in which she established a loving relationship between herself and the Princess. When the Princess settled down to watch the peasant *pas de deux*, Giselle stands at the cottage door, her eyes never for a moment leaving Bathilde's face; at the same time she caresses her cheek with the necklace she has just received. I think this is a beautiful insight, establishing one of the central ironies of the ballet—that a girl of a feudal society is to be betrayed, although unknowingly, by someone far above her station and one whom, despite this, she has come to love so securely.

In the second act Makarova achieved the purest imaginable classical style, grafted to the softer romanticism of the period before Petipa, each seen together as a whole. When she danced it was as if the air vibrated musically as she moved within it, like the strings of a harp that she touched magically in passing. This was true musicality, seen in terms of phrasing, the distribution of stress, the varying of pace and dynamics within the whole of the dance. How far indeed is this from Gautier's pretty ballet, yet how one wishes he could have written of it and made it immortal, this imperious statement of a classic art.

Makarova's performance in *La Sylphide* shows us another aspect of Romanticism, and gives a remarkable insight into her almost uncanny sense of period style, even within two ballets both created in the same tradition over a hundred years ago. At once, both in her dancing and in the interpretation of the role, she distinguishes between the pretty sentiment of the Sylphide and the tragedy of Giselle with the most delicate appreciation of the difference between the romanticism of Bournonville and the classicism of Perrot as seen by Petipa. Her Sylphide is a page of history as well as a work of art.

This Sylphide is half spirit, half child, wilful, impetuous and sly, full of sweet mockery, tenderness and guile. To watch her in the first act indicate to James her falling tears is to find a perfect balance between Victorian sentiment and true grief, as touching and poignant as music from a spinet or a harpsichord. Here is all the sweet romance of a Valentine, now decorated by appropriate tears, a world of loving sighs. It is not pastiche but recreation, a lost world recalled in her huge sad eyes.

In the second act her dancing opens to the music as some mysterious night-flower, the symbol of her art, might open to the moon. I shall always remember how in one solo two single turns *en attitude* formed themselves with a kind of piercing beauty, pale and translucent like an arctic rose. The air supported her, this stranger to our mortal earth.

Makarova's dancing is so intricately woven from the music that it seems to be embroidered from it, each musical phrase a silken thread. The resultant picture is like a Victorian keepsake, so pretty, so delicate in outline that it belongs to an age far distant from our own. Her sense of period is impeccable; this portrait becomes a sublime evocation of Lucile Grahn, the first Sylphide at the Theatre Royal nearly a hundred and fifty years ago, whom the critic Jules Janin described as 'a beautiful person who dances like the singing of a bird'.

Few scenes in contemporary ballet can be so moving as the death of this Sylphide—her taut, stricken body, arched in a mortal anguish; the shudder of her last expiring sigh; the emptiness of her eyes that were once the harbingers of such beauty and such high romance. It is a moment of extraordinary pathos: it seemed as if a child had died, the merry and beguiling spirit with her mocking eyes now no more substantial than twilight drifting to the earth.

One is astonished how in every performance of the same ballet a different dramatic weight is given to each scene, as the ballerina continues to explore its emotional possibilities, so that one particular section of the ballet will be examined with a far greater intensity than on an earlier night. Innumerable details will be added, new phrasing to the music, an altered balance of emphasis in the *enchaînement*, a fresh insight into character or its relationship to the other roles, in much the same manner as a painter will concentrate on a particular section of his canvas or a certain aspect of its design. We are thus able to watch the free play of the artist's imagination, the dance as a creative act.

On two successive performances of *Romeo and Juliet* with the Royal Ballet in July, 1975 we were able to study the growth and elaboration of the choreographic ideas, at one performance concentrated on the ballroom scene, at the other on the bedchamber scenes of the third act. Here the images of grief were so carved out of the music that even in moments of repose the line of the arms and torso were made to speak with an unsurpassed eloquence, tragedy expressed in a series of related designs. The balance of lines and angles was so conceived that each image was as articulate as a soliloquy, the verse for a moment held and transfigured in a single pose.

It would be invidious to try and analyse these poses in which the ballerina, with her astounding insight into the nature of plastic imagery as an expression of a hidden emotional life, encloses whole poems in the curve of her arms; sufficient to say that they are her own vision, her own truth. No ballerina will ever be able to imitate Natalia Makarova any more than they could the art of Anna Pavlova. Talent can be imitated but not genius. And this I would define as the intensity and originality of the creative act. In Emerson's words it 'adorns nature with a new thing'.

In the ballroom scene of *Romeo and Juliet* her dancing is not only an interpretation of the growth of love in all its stages, it is for us a direct experience of that love in its essential nature. All that might come between us and the ballerina—all artifice, all fantasy—is in some way eliminated. It is a love discovered on first sight, the meeting of one glance, then growing to its final ecstatic realisation when she seems to dance within a dream, dazed like one possessed, now beyond the reach of our mortal earth. In one extraordinary moment in this scene Makarova reaches forwards with her arms like a sleep-walker, as if to touch the vision she sees before her eyes, to feel it, know its shape, as someone blind might seek with his hands to grasp the empty air. It is as if she gazed on the face of love itself, seen 'as in a glass darkly', so that she tries to clear away with her hands the shadows that lie across it.

In the balcony scene the music is lit by moonlight, full of the sounds and scents of a summer night. Her heart throbs from within it, pulses to the rhythm of her blood. Here the dance ripples and shimmers like the tide that turns beneath the moon. It is enchanted, where the surrender to love is complete and there is no reason, no logic in it any more. It is ecstatic, a kind of madness. All the abandonment of love is in her dancing, the obliteration of self in a moment's total surrender, the daring that will risk all in one final utterance.

The last *pas de deux* with Paris is a duet faint from a mortal sickness; in it is a sense of revulsion from which the defeated spirit turns, shuddering and afraid. Now her body faints, sinks into a final surrender; it is bereft of life, of vital movement, of any hope. Now she expresses a misery that has not even the will to despair, a kind of hideous echo of all that she has danced before, all the hopes now defaced, the love disfigured, and the shame.

There is a profound irony in that the music here from the moment of the entry of Juliet's parents with Paris is a recapitulation of part of the music from the joyous ballroom scene. Juliet's *pas de deux* with Paris is a sad echo of the same dance then, even to the gesture of her arms reaching upwards that is linked to the same little curling phrase in the music, but now her body droops most piteously and the gesture is no longer one of happiness but despair.

I remember and see them now, those moments of stillness, perfect in line, emotion sculptured in a single pose: the moment when she first greets Romeo, her eyes huge and awakening with love; the moment when he leaves her after their bridal night, and she is alone on the empty stage—a pose that in an instant accepts all, wills all the consequences of her loving; when her father flings her to the ground after her rejection of Paris and she reaches in despair to the empty bed, then turns her face away, her arms limp at her sides. I remember her in flight to Friar Laurence, her cloak, flame-like, fluttering behind her; or beneath the balcony, moving across the stage like reflected light. I see her now in the first scene—the wide leaps, the little runs on *pointes* when she is suddenly so secretive and alone and which we are to see again when she breaks free from Paris, chooses her own solitude, her unspoken despair. All the stages of human love are in this performance. Her arms speak; her body is a chorus of voices.

If as a result of her own individuality and the free creative movement of her imagination, she is able to startle herself as well as the audience, so much the better. I am reminded of Julien Green's fine remark in his Journal: 'In art, truth lies in surprising.' So with Makarova we are surprised by truth seen as if for the first time in the astonishment of great art.

It is not only in modern works that Makarova is able to make an image leap out of the music, to summarize an emotion in a single design. Her dancing in the second act of *Swan Lake* is enclosed by images that frame the whole scene in two statements of imperious art. The first is at her entry, when suddenly she is there, as if Odette had swooped down, alighted in a moment from the sky. This wide leap with her arms outspread like beating wings is almost savage, elemental; she is a creature of instinct, wild and untamed, come out of the night. At that moment there is no trace of the enchanted princess within her: she is Rothbart's creature, irredeemably lost in his terrible dream. It is an extraordinary insight where one can almost hear the creak of damp pinions, the rustle of great wings. Then she approaches the Prince and in one glance that has in it both terror and an anguished appeal she meets his gaze, though she cannot hold it, for her instinct draws her back into the darkness. While he still clasps her, she turns her head away to look almost with longing to the world from which she came. We can see how the young girl hidden within her enchantment can only with pain emerge from her hiding, to face the realities of love that will set her free. How profound a symbol this is of love at whose glance at first we draw away, knowing by instinct the perilous journey on which we are now embarked.

*Swan Lake* is a legend of the pain and the delight of first love, found within the confused dark of instinct and drawn forth, beautiful and unsullied like a lost princess. In less than thirty seconds of dancing Natalia Makarova summarizes the whole theme, the central struggle between instinct and will that is at the heart of our emotional life. It is an insight not only into the music and into the choreography but deep within her own nature and our own.

At the end of this act Rothbart appears and as the chord of music sounds in which he calls her back, her whole body convulses; the shoulders arch, the arms constrict in terror. It is as if she had been impaled by some deadly arrow, struck mortally to the heart. In that moment Odette, the princess, is lost; the terrible transformation in nature is to begin again. Her back to the audience, she glides away and in the line of her arms, the carriage of her head, we can see with what reluctance she fights against the spell which holds her powerless. Caught between the Prince and Rothbart for a moment she seems to be torn asunder; then she vanishes and the triumph of evil has been attained. No other ballerina in my experience has been able

*Les Biches* (Royal Ballet) and *Jardin aux Lilas*
with Gayle Young (American Ballet Theatre)

(previous page)
*Giselle* with
Mikhail Baryshnikov
(American Ballet Theatre)

to achieve this sense of transformation that in her performance encloses the act within a single design. It is the transfiguring of art into the expression of visionary truth.

Although I had been down to Plymouth to see Makarova when she danced with the Royal Ballet in their 'Big Top' during the summer of 1976, I had not realized how much her art had developed until I watched her again at Covent Garden in November of that year. It is true that at Plymouth, dancing in *Swan Lake* and *Romeo and Juliet*, she appeared more serene and self-assured than I had known her in the past, making experiments in the dance with a kind of insouciance and daring quite new to me, but it was not until she returned to Covent Garden that one was aware of a new splendour.

This was particularly noticeable in her first performances of *Swan Lake*, a ballet in which like *Giselle* she finds an inexhaustible treasury of new meanings. Her dancing had in the second act gained a new lyricism, so that each movement was shaped into soft cadences, drifting like the fall of snow. The coldness of the classical line had in some mysterious way become blurred and softened into a kind of misty reflection of the music, so that she achieved a fresh vision of the role, seen now with a new tenderness that was at once both rapt and serene. It was like the dancing of a sigh.

The profoundly romantic interpretation of this act now stood in greater contrast to the clarity and brilliance of the third act; here the romantic dream had suddenly become vibrant with life and the intensity of experience, as if it were the fulfilment in reality of what had long been known in the imagination, thus linking the two acts into a complete allegory of human love. It was a glimpse not only into the symbolism of the ballet, but into the experience of love as the fulfilment of the ideal in terms of physical passion.

These three performances proved once again the extraordinary richness of her creative imagination, since they differed so much in emotional tone. In the second and third performances Makarova strove for even greater unity between the white acts by showing how grief can darken with experience into despair. Odette in the second act is shown in a mood of tender melancholy, a creature of brooding romance whose innocence protects her from knowledge of the deepest sorrow. Her instinctive nature, symbolised by the swan, is transfigured by love into a truly human passion; but she has as yet no knowledge of betrayal, of all experiences the one that brings a woman to full maturity through suffering. In the final act she has discovered this; now the dancing is weightier, set in colder lines, framed within a desolating splendour only hinted at before. Grief has been transformed into an elegy of hopeless love, sorrow brought to the icy depths of despair, pathos grown into tragedy. The soft lyricism of the second act is now replaced by a marbled grandeur of movement, the full richness of the imperial style; the lost girl is transformed into the tragic woman. In some ways indeed she is closer to Odile—the woman in thrall to a hopeless love—than she is to the early Odette, so that the whole ballet is carried forward in one great statement about the nature of a woman's love and her growth in self-understanding through grief and betrayal.

These sublime transitions were shown in dancing of such musical comprehension that one felt no note of the score, no line or curve of melody had been neglected. One tiny example of this—gone in a few seconds but rooted imperishably in memory—was how before her solo in the second act began Makarova shaped the line of a small *glissando* of the harp in the curving movement of her arm, so that it seemed she plucked the music out of the air and drew it like a glittering filament downwards in a single sweep, to rest with the melody at the still point of her repose. As she danced she gathered the music around her and set it free, falling away into silence at the end of each phrase, those tiny pulses of stillness across which the dance is carried that mark the refinements of her style. Of all ballerinas she is the most musical I have ever known in that she sets before us the architecture of the music, each curve or fading line, like some ancient palace glimpsed within a dream.

Even more amazing were the three entirely different Odiles she created at these performances. Their qualities were not shown to us in terms of mime but in the type of movement, the most subtle gradations in musical phrasing and differences in shading the classical line. This is not easy to describe: one might say they were differences resulting from hard or soft lines set against the music, in the sudden brilliant shaping of a pose, or a manner of growing more softly into it, as though the music coaxed her into the heart of its stillness. It was in the manner she entered the dance, either impetuously or hesitantly, either with flamboyance or a most touching reticence; how she drew herself together, like the taking of a breath by a singer, before the first phrase was formed. One of the distinctive qualities of Makarova's dancing is how she enters each phrase of the music and the dance; sometimes it is impetuous, at others hesitant, or again with a smooth flowing confidence. Her dancing is like a greeting she gives to each musical phrase, so that in her movements we catch the altered cadences of the human voice set against the curve of the melodic line. Her dance is song to which the music is accompaniment.

It was through such dancing that we could study these separate Odiles. The first, as she had described it to me, was the portrait of mature love; the second a study in cruel sensuality; the third, a picture of the troubled heart. It was possible to see how the ideas she had suggested to me some months earlier, that were described in the previous chapter, as possible lines for developing the characterisation of Odile had been very considerably extended. This is merely one example of how every role is always under scrutiny and never set in any final pattern. If she could come to the end of new interpretations of her greatest roles, I believe she would abandon them on the instant. I recall her saying to me once, almost in panic, 'What happens if one day I can't find anything new in *Giselle*?' Knowing something of the richness of her imagination, I feel there is no danger of that.

If the first of these Odiles had been very much as she had discussed them with me, for her second performance she returned to the evil aspect of the character though in a manner very different from the traditional playing of the role. This Odile mocked the dancing of Odette in a series of savage distortions, taking the poses from the earlier *pas de deux*, hardening them, sharpening the lines, thrusting them almost brutally against the music. Here the luckless Siegfried was crushed, overpowered; her passion for him barely concealed the hatred that lay beneath it. She was not as in some earlier performances a spirit of evil; here the dancing was entirely physical, combining flamboyant sensuality with a calculated malignancy.

It could be objected—and, indeed, I have heard Makarova make the same observation—that such an Odile would be more likely to cause the spineless Prince to take to his heels than embrace any marriage vows; better indeed to settle down with a tigress in quiet domesticity, or share one's repose with a lioness. However, never did she lose for an instant the elegance of the classical style or the aristocracy of her Kirov schooling. This was the *danse d'école*, even if portrayed by a merciless harpie. Makarova knows that I do not like this kind of interpretation of Odile, and I hope she felt the cold breath of my disapproval blowing from the upper reaches of the house; yet it was stunningly, almost contemptuously danced, as though she flung the audience a bone—one, moreover, ripped from the thigh of the critic who had been imperceptive enough to castigate her former Odile as lacking in a sense of evil.

The final Odile of this astounding triology was again different, in my view by far the most subtle of all. Here she tried to become Odette again, now seen not in terms of mockery or scorn, her innocence caricatured, but in a mood almost of longing as if she sought to recall her own youth, the child touched by first love. The style was softer, glowing in its own radiance, no longer with the brilliance of a diamond but with the sheen of a black pearl. The dance was wavering, hesitant, seemingly lit intermittently by flashes of light, indicating the unequal beat of the restless, troubled heart. It was something new, daring, something she had never attempted before—this portrait of a woman torn between a yearning for love and an inability, because of the power Rothbart exerted over her, to express it. In the *pas de deux* she would hesitate a fraction, seem for a moment to draw back, before she entered Siegfried's arms; one had the sense of a curious unease within her dancing, an uncertainty what role to play, a terrible reluctance to commit herself to love.

This, I think, is very remarkable: to show us Odile under the power of Rothbart, so that she is forced against her will to destroy Siegfried, the man whom she so yearns to love. Rothbart might even stand for that darkness within herself—whether one calls it original sin or the corruption of innocence through vice—which holds her back from ever being able to embrace real love again. It seems that the power of the spell Rothbart imposes each time he calls her to him during the *pas de deux* weakens when she is with Siegfried again, as if love slowly began to erode the force of evil. She goes to him from Rothbart at first harshly, cruelly, but with a cruelty which is not her own, yet slowly her movements soften so that she is now herself again. Seeing this, Rothbart calls her back; hesitantly she returns to Siegfried, now distanced from her love, more open to Rothbart's curse. Here the conflict between Odette, Rothbart and the Prince, shown in the second act, is again repeated, now in the person of Odile, caught in the same struggle between the powers of love and those of darkness, in itself the central allegory of the greatest works of art.

It is a performance of extraordinary daring, even, one might say, metaphysical, or—as that sounds affected—spiritual, where the inner conflicts in human nature between the will to do evil and the longing to do good exist in a continual tension that is at the heart of both theology and of metaphysics. Odile is forced to do evil, even while she longs to love, and the tragedy of this act is carried through into the final scene by the lakeside where Odette is become the abandoned Odile, knowing now the full desolation of what she has done.

It is not possible, in considering her various portrayals of Odette-Odile to say that any one of them is definitive. I made such a mistake when once, as I have mentioned, I discussed 'her Giselle' with her, only to have my wrist slapped. Instead each is an unfinished story to which she is always adding a new chapter, or setting the characters in a new landscape. One of Makarova's relaxations is in painting, but I am sure she never lets the canvas dry; she is always eager to begin again, to catch the moment and make it imperishable in her art.

# SEVEN

# The Outer World

## OTHER ROLES

TO TURN FROM Makarova's interpretations of the major roles to those in shorter ballets is to find that the scale and intensity of her performances are in no way diminished. She paints large and in detail, even on the smallest canvas, whether it be a one-act ballet or even an isolated *pas de deux*. Neither in life nor her art has she any time for small talk. Natalia Makarova is only interested in new frontiers, particularly those that are distant from her and which only she can attain.

The highest form of the dance is that which speaks to us in terms of visual metaphor, a series of highly-compressed images like those of poetry. It is a language closer to us than words, as close as music, and this is the language of her dance. These images are not confined to dance-dramas like *Manon* and *Romeo and Juliet*, but can be found, if the ballerina has the sensitivity to explore them, in all works that are more than the stringing together of academic steps. They speak of a world of mysterious relationships, as we can discover from the works of Robbins, Tetley, Bruce and van Manen who have found in the so-called abstract ballet a truer means of communication than any to be discovered in the dance-drama.

In the slow movement of MacMillan's *Concerto*, for example, Makarova gives us an extraordinary picture that is like the dawn of a new creation, the first exploration, at once spiritual and tactile, of her own nature, the mystery of her own being. Almost fearfully she begins to awaken, to sense her own consciousness, to feel the movement of her limbs. She stretches out her arms as though she groped towards the mysterious light that opens around her, the dawn of that first day when Eve awoke in the symbolic garden and knew her own being, stranger, more mysterious, more beautiful than all that lay around her. In this wonderful *pas de deux* her dancing reaches a spiritual intensity that is hers alone to understand. It is more than the dawn of creation; it is the awakening of the heart.

In MacMillan's *Song of the Earth*, a fine example of a modern plotless ballet, Makarova moves in a region she has made particularly her own. Here is a sense of loneliness, of vast solitude, as if she drifted in and out of our world like a ghost, alone and vulnerable, forever a little apart. In *Song of the Earth* she faces the last and most solitary of all our encounters, our meeting with death; here she accepts all, without love, without fear, in the icy twilight of that music's farewell. The music encloses her as she turns her face to the void, reaches to it as if for one last dark kiss.

Similarly in *Checkmate*, which she danced for the first time at Sadler's Wells on 6th October, 1975, Makarova composed one of her most extraordinary portraits, a dazzling glimpse into a surrealist dream. Her Black Queen is like a fragment from a nightmare where chess pieces grow to fantastic proportions and dance in the eerie light of a cold sun. This is an inhuman creature, exotic, sinuous and enigmatic, in some manner almost oriental, as if the formal language of the classical dance were spoken in another tongue, more primitive, more elemental than our own.

She has her own logic, secret and instinctive, refined with a precision quite alien to any human scale of thought or feeling. If a chess piece could think or act, it would act so, but in no way does it relate to ourselves; this is another order of being, a nature that is subtle yet curiously mechanistic—a thing of logic yet devoid of a soul. Primitive nature is seen contained only by reason, but never for a moment is it tamed or modified by any human heart. It is a performance of strange daring, a leap into a world of terrible logic, more cruel even than our own.

Or so at first it seemed. But then as one looked closer below this flawless surface one could see flickering, like the fire that burns at the heart of a diamond, a tiny glimmer of human warmth. When she first encounters the Red Knight she is suddenly attracted, observing him with curiosity and a kind of pity. Then one notices how she extinguishes that small flame in her heart as their mortal conflict begins. Yet for a moment after his death it is as if she cannot endure what she has done: the tension of her body when she stands, isolated from the other dancers and alone, begins to slacken, to fall into broken lines, and it is with a terrible effort that she conquers this weakness which seems to threaten her repose, to make her human and vulnerable, a part of our imperfect world.

This sense of inner conflict, where her humanity is for a moment glimpsed and then so brutally extinguished by an act of will, adds an extraordinary depth to Makarova's portrait. One realises how near the Black Queen has come to us, one like us who suffers and lets fall her tears. Then the will is seen to conquer; bleak and implacable, she can resume her reign, and the Red King be destroyed with all the cold precision of an empty, abandoned heart.

It is fascinating to watch a ballerina of such warm humanity portray a role that is constructed so much against her own nature, as one was to notice again when she danced the part of the chilly Girl in Blue in Nijinska's *Les Biches* for the first time at Covent Garden in December, 1975. Here was shown a figure both asexual and lonely, an ice maiden, her eyes splintered with frozen tears. Nijinska's choreography is eerily two-dimensional, drawn in bleak lines and harsh angularities, and it is this sense of the cold, unloved heart, a kind of huge world-weariness, that is so marvellously evoked in Makarova's performance.

One feels the Girl in Blue has experienced everything, known too much, and that she is sated and weary with the long loneliness of her life; yet—and this is so remarkable in Makarova's reading—she gives the impression also of an extreme vulnerability that she guards with icy glances and disdainful smiles. It is, maybe, the solitude of a huge and now spent self-love that so imprisons her in joyless isolation. Indeed few among Makarova's gallery of portraits are so curious, so enigmatic and so bleakly observed as this cold being, secret in her loveless repose.

No greater contrast to this can be found than in MacMillan's *Elite Syncopations* which she danced for the first time in 1975. Her interpretation, as she told me, was to be 'vulgarly sophisticated', as if performed by a film vamp of the Twenties. Here she wore a red top hat at a jaunty angle, as if to the manner born. One could not imagine such frivolity at the Kirov, where they would certainly not allow their *prima ballerina* to dance in so undignified a romp. But Makarova is devoid of pomposity, given to moods of almost child-like high spirits that gain perfect release in ballets of this kind. It is sad that we have not been able to see her in more comic works, as there is a whole side of her nature at present neglected by modern choreographers—the sense of fun, the jauntiness and love of ridiculous situations—and one hopes that soon this will be allowed to go free to her amusement and our delight.

Natalia Makarova made her first appearance in Glen Tetley's great ballet, *Voluntaries*, in December, 1976. Here was a work she greatly admired, one perfectly suited to the intense emotional commitment of her dancing and to her almost orchestral range of movement. This first performance took me by surprise, as happens so often with her dancing, since it was different from what I had envisaged it to be. I expected something heroic, a huge defiance in the face of death, a great sweep of tragic dance. Instead she spoke so quietly in her dancing, a statement that was both personal and intimate, a kind of simplicity when one had expected baroque magnificence. 'I grieve so,' she seemed to say. 'In this way, like yours, my heart breaks.' Yet it was not only her grief, it was all our grieving—the loneliness of it, the solitude, the terrible sense of finality that seems to crush us beyond all thought of re-birth. The dancing was like a series of broken sobs. Sudden constrictions of grief were followed by moments of hopeless lassitude when the body sinks upon itself in a huge solitude.

Makarova did not, like her predecessors in the role, blaze in sudden defiance; instead, at the close of the ballet, she forced herself with an agonising effort to live again, to pick up the broken threads of her life, reaching outwards with her arms as if to touch an unseen face that would lead her out of the darkness of her despair. I found in it more truth than I could endure; indeed I wanted some artifice, some theatricalism to ease the pain she forced us to share.

Such a performance makes great demands on an audience who have not the courage to follow her across a landscape of such terrible desolation. It makes us face the pain, the loneliness and the sense of loss that is so much a part of living, while we are invited to share a belief that to live in defiance of our grief is likely to be beyond our strength. Makarova has, both personally and as an artist, not only a deep humility that refuses to pretend she is stronger, more noble and defiant in grief than we are ourselves, but she is also supremely courageous as an artist in that she gives herself totally, with an almost painful honesty, even if this is to reveal her own weaknesses, her troubled and vulnerable heart.

In the second performance of *Voluntaries* Makarova shifted the emphasis in her interpretation. Possibly influenced by the death that day of Benjamin Britten which had caused the work to be danced as a tribute to him at the beginning of the programme, she brought a far greater emphasis to the other central theme of the ballet— the triumph of the creative spirit over death. Here within the grief there was also exultation, an affirmation of life over all those forces that seek to destroy it. Now the dance was less intimate; it spoke in a language more universal, and was thus expressed with greater force, in wider sweeps of movement, in a broader clarity of line. It was, in fact, what I had expected the first performance to have been, not a development of this but rather a new approach to the role, seeking within it different responses and wider harmonies.

During this same season Makarova also appeared in Jerome Robbins' *Dances at a Gathering* for the first time, and in Hans van Manen's *Adagio Hammerklavier*. She has great admiration for Robbins' work, and ever since she had attended the first performance of *Dances at a Gathering* at Covent Garden, she had longed to dance in this ballet where the poetic and lyrical choreography with its free open lines and sense almost of improvisation exactly suited her own style.

From her entry in the beautiful *pas de deux* she caught instantly the mood of ardent, awakening youth, the first troubled Spring of the heart, so that she let her movements float across the music as clouds might be carried over the sky. The dance was rapt, serene, wondering; it was like the first encounter with a newly-discovered world in all the mystery and delight of youth. Each phrase of the dance came to her unexpectedly like a glimpse into an unknown land. Never have I known her to look younger; she was a girl of sixteen, seeking her way among new emotions, tiny flutters of the heart.

The dance had an extraordinary fragility; indeed at times it appeared almost tentative, sketched in such pure and delicate lines against the music, drifting as on the currents of soft and moving air, the small, fickle winds of early summer. It was the recollection of childhood, those first wondering hours when she ran through the woods, a child on holiday in Russia. It was life as a child sees it—in part a game, in part an exploration of her own secret emotions.

When she danced in a later section with her companions—each

repeating in turn the same sequence of steps—she followed them in a *grand jeté* with a sudden jubilation, like a child who almost defiantly shows how she can leap higher than any of her friends, move swifter than all her rivals. It was a little display of pride and emulation, a sudden impudence, as if to say to them that anything they could do she could do better—a rush of self-assurance, enchanting in its child-like vanity like the snub of a nose.

When, in the last *pas de deux* she is caught suddenly in an emotion deeper than that of flirtation or coquetry, so that she fears the loneliness, the uncertainty of love, she drew away from her partner with a curious impulsiveness as a child might run away from a kiss. It is too early, her heart seemed to say, I am not ready for love, and I am afraid. Here the dance was seen as an encounter with a frightening reality, so that she breaks off abruptly leaving her partner standing there, amazed.

Somehow Makarova was able throughout the ballet to show in a single hour the long awakening of adolescence from wonder, rivalry, and coquetry towards love, and the fearful recognition that youth is fading even as we chase it in its flight; that age will come and grief and death, so that at the end the dancers bow to one another with a sad understanding and go off slowly into their unknown future in a mood of quiet resignation, for the long bright summer of their playing is over.

She had made this exquisite and delicate ballet into the story of her own youth, the end of that youth, and her serene acceptance of all the griefs that waited for her beyond its enchanted garden. She had caught each mood and built them into an allegory as all great dancing is; for it is like this to be young, like this to know the ending of one's youth and to accept it quietly but with a little pain. Her dancing in this ballet is like her own autobiography—the story of her heart, but made universal, reaching with the sad and sometimes wry concern that is so much a part of her own character, across to each of us and greeting us in a moment's recognition. In few other roles have I been so aware of her humanity, the depths of her compassion, not just for us but that more difficult compassion, the one we show for ourselves.

Although Makarova recognises the brilliance and originality of Hans van Manen's choreography, she did not feel at ease in his *Adagio Hammerklavier* as she had done in Robbins' masterpiece. I think it is possibly because the dance images are too remote, almost too intellectual, for an artist of such rare humanity; they separated her from her audience so that she could not feel them with that immediacy which is one of her most marked characteristics as a dancer. Yet I found her performance, cold and objective as the choreography demanded, one of an almost unearthly beauty. I have never known her so far away, or been conscious of the icy distances that held us apart from her world. At the very beginning of the ballet she is carried off the stage by her partner in one long, curving lift, so typical of the choreographer, her arms opening skyward, so that it was as if she reached to clutch the stars. It was more than an image of yearning; it was more one of the most absolute desolation, she alone and abandoned on the empty earth.

Hans van Manen's choreography is magnificently devised as a contrast between broken, almost grotesque movement and the purest classical lines, so that each image is formed as if from shattered fragments, bringing form and order out of distortion and ugliness. I find it a profound statement of the classical dance in all its wide symbolism, how from chaos is created harmony, the beauty of the willed design seen as the working of the spirit upon inchoate matter. One recalls St. Augustine's great remark that 'beauty is the splendour of order'.

It may be that this cold, intellectual work, that in my view so exactly mirrors the thought behind Beethoven's vision in the slow movement of the Hammerklavier sonata, is not one that appeals to the ardent temperament of Natalia Makarova, for it is not concerned with the movements of the heart but with a statement about classicism as an expression of the creative spirit. The ballet is like the working out of a series of syllogisms in movement, and she needs something more human than this. She danced in the ballet with that wonderful purity of style, the nobility in the shaping of each image that belongs only to the greatest of Kirov dancers, yet it never belonged to her as her greatest dances belong as part of her own nature. If she seemed far away from us, so the choreography had distanced her from her own emotions.

Of all great choreographers van Manen has the least feminine imagination; apart from the works of Ninette de Valois, I can recall no ballets so objective, so impersonally wrought: they are like sculptures in music, exploration of the space around the dancer rather than any expression of her inner life. I think this is why Makarova can admire them, but why she cannot love them as she does the ballets of Jerome Robbins for they do not speak directly to her heart. Unlike most of the critics, I find this a noble and profound work, yet I was not happy to see her in it because I do not like her so far away. I love in her dancing the nearness of her spirit, and this could not be found here.


During the 1977 season with Nureyev at the London Coliseum she was to dance for the first time in Flemming Flindt's curious ballet, *The Lesson*, based on a play by Ionesco. It is an old-fashioned work in some respects, originally designed for television, but the role of the pupil at her class with a mad ballet teacher gave Makarova an opportunity very much to her taste. She is quite willing in a relaxed mood to tear a passion to tatters; what is so delightful about her performance in *The Lesson* is that she does it with something like a wide grin. One is reminded how Wilde said that the fate of Little Nell moved him to tears of laughter, and the unfortunate pupil in this ballet suffers a fate equally melodramatic and not a little absurd.

Makarova creates an adorable ballet student—wilful, impetuous, high-spirited and exasperating. There is more than a trace of the spoiled child in her own character, the demands of a fierce will, and this she exploits to dazzling effect in *The Lesson*. It is at first very funny, this impetuous demanding little madam, so pretty with her cropped hair, so eager to get on with her class, so disrespectful in some ways to her professor, a creature of moods and barely-concealed tantrums. One wonders how much of young Natalia Makarova is preserved here—the strong willed young girl at the Kirov, so pliable in some ways, so exasperatingly stubborn in others. I feel there is a great deal, remembering the child who put a hedgehog in her mother's bed.

Of course *The Lesson* is a creaking little melodrama, and she and Nureyev played it with their tongues in their cheeks, catching the true zany spirit of Ionesco exactly, so complex a mixture of farce and terror. And when the moment came, her terror was real. The maddeningly spoiled child in an instant grew up, in an instant confronted death with a huge realisation of its anguish, made more startling because of the earlier playing of the role. To encompass broad comedy, farce and horror in a single performance is no small challenge for a ballerina; and she who lives on challenges at every moment was not likely to refuse it.

On the same night she danced Flemming Flindt's elegant reconstruction of a *pas de deux* from Bournonville's *The Toreador*. At once she caught the muted, compact Danish style, adapting the more flowing and open Kirov technique to this small, rather pretty world of movement; she might have been a little provincial dancer in nineteenth century Copenhagen who had never even heard of Petipa and the Imperial Russian Ballet. She painted the music like a water-colour of old Spain.

After the noble classical dancing in her own production of *La Bayadère*, Makarova was able during the following season by Ballet Theatre to make the huge transition to the elemental world of Glen Tetley's *Sacre du Printemps*. The finest version of this ballet

*Voluntaries* with David Wall (Royal Ballet)

*Le Sacre du Printemps* with Clark Tippet (American Ballet Theatre)

*Checkmate* (Sadler's Wells Royal Ballet)

I have seen, it was dominated by two fierce performances by herself and Baryshnikov of quite shattering impact, setting the audience aroar in a manner I have not heard since the first night of Roland Petit's *Carmen*, some twenty-five years ago.

Tetley's ballet has the ambiguity in its symbolism, the many different layers of meaning, that belong to the finest works in the theatre; each member of the audience will find his own particular truth in it, images that have a particular meaning for himself alone. Its structure is, however, very simple in that the traditional role of the Chosen Maiden is shared between a male and female dancer who seek for re-birth in terms of sexual love. The dancers continually aspire upwards, even while they are weighted down to the earth; the sense of the primitive and the spiritual, the animal and the human, exists in a duality that is continually explored in the dance.

Makarova shared the female role with Martine van Hamel, a fine dancer with a bold, authoritative way of moving and a commanding presence. No two interpretations could have been more different: while van Hamel triumphed in her sexuality, so tyat her partner was almost her victim, Makarova brought to the role a most touching vision of defeated innocence. She was the victim, a creature used by men, passive in a mood of total acceptance. Before the great *pas de deux* with her enigmatic lover, she stands in dejection, shoulders hunched, her body listless, eyes vacant and sad; the idea of the maiden chosen for sacrifice is enclosed in her listless body, arms hanging to her sides like those of a broken marionette.

In the *pas de deux* her body is curved in a piteous search for flight; vainly she aspires upwards, seeming to claw the air with tattered pinions. One feels the torn flesh, the small poor bones piercing the skin. She is like a maimed bird, her arms its broken wings. In one beautiful image she flings her body back so that she falls in an arch across her partner; it is like the spasm of a caged bird flinging itself against the bars. Even as her body is drawn downwards, it yearns for flight; sometimes she seems on the verge of taking wing, then sinks again in an attitude of huge exhaustion and defeat.

Crouched like a foetus, or arched as in a constriction of birth, it seems the dance is torn from the womb of the earth, screaming like the mandrake root wrenched from the ground. It is dancing stripped of all artifice, as if each sinew were exposed, so that we can sense the muscles stretched beneath the flesh, feel the curve of those exhausted wings. The extraordinary suppleness of her body, coupled with her instinctive sense of line, make this performance the most physical I have ever seen her give; it is at once both sensual and despairing, as if the imprisoned spirit sought to tear itself from the flesh.

No contrast could have been greater than between this performance and her *pas de deux, Other Dances,* composed by Jerome Robbins for herself and Mikhail Baryshnikov. It is a kind of coda to *Dances at a Gathering,* quieter, cooler, less deeply involved, in which Robbins asks his dancers to sketch their images over the cool surface of the music in a mood that is almost improvisory. They walk quite naturally to the part of the stage where they are to begin their dance, and when one leaves the other says farewell in the most casual way imaginable, or calls her back as if they were alone, amusing themselves in the studio or after rehearsal.

Makarova's dancing is child-like, almost whimsical, toying with the music, adjusting it as she might try on a new dress in front of the mirror. One sees a child alone—the same child, indeed, who watched herself weep in front of the glass—lost in her secret pleasures, even a little guileful, rather sly; perhaps, one thinks, she has no right to be here, flirting with the music, coaxing it along like a reluctant friend who is not perhaps quite so eager to join in the game. I recall how André Levinson described Anna Pavlova's dance in *Mort du Cygne* as being like an improvisation, and Makarova gives exactly that impression; in her opening solo, she takes three small steps, then pauses for a fraction, poised giddily on the edge of the music, seeking in her mind the step she will decide to dance.

In a curious way it sets both the choreographer and the audience in the position of onlookers, intruders in a private encounter between herself and the music. It is enchanting at the end to see her fling the last notes of music into the air in one impetuous gesture of her arms; it is as if these final phrases were captive doves she flung free into the sky, into a wide silence. Natalia Makarova told me much about her childhood; but I understood it better here when she danced it.

Makarova's own nature is, of course, the source of her huge artistic range, for she is, as I have tried to indicate in the first chapter, highly volatile, imaginative and sensitive. It is exactly that vividness of sensation, an almost physical feel for mood and atmosphere, that is the source of her inventiveness as an artist. Yet in her performances this rich emotional life is never allowed to get out of control, however daring are the risks she takes, as in *Romeo and Juliet* and *Manon*, because she is also logical and highly intelligent, so being able to study her technique in an analytical manner.

It is a very simple truth that I have been circling so warily: she dances as she dances because she is the person that she is. To see her dance is to see her whole; to try and examine the quality of her dancing, springing as it does from such a complex emotional life, is just about as easy as trying to separate the strands of a rainbow. As we have seen in the previous chapter she is not concerned with artifice or theatricalism; she is concerned only with the truth of the emotions she explores. To this only she will respond. In her art she gives herself entirely in all the subtleties of her inner life since it is an expression of her being. We share the same humanity that is in her dancing in all its truth.

There is a kind of defiance in the greatest dancing that snatches with such fiery pride these sudden images from the void, and fixes them in one moment of astounding repose, as if they were to stand forever like sculptures in imperishable stone. It is no wonder that

Natalia Makarova is so impatient for each performance to begin, or seeks in her life for such intensity of experience, for the solitary world of her art has been reached after the troubled journey I have in part described and its rewards are so brief and so uncertain. Like all great dancers she leaves nothing behind of her impermanent day, only words like these which like sullen mourners are all that remain to recall its passing.

I have always tried in books on the ballet to find in words— whether my own or those of another writer—parallel images to those of the dance. None that I know are more beautiful, or more appropriate to her art, than these lines from a poem by Iain Crichton Smith:

It is not the image of the beautiful

makes it so, simply as in a mirror,
but its fadingness, as on the ice
the deer might suddenly slip, go suddenly under,

their balance being precarious. It is this,
that makes her beautiful, she who now obscures
unconscious heavens with her conscious ray,

is concourse of bright flesh, sad, is remembering
herself so going, so implacable,
her failing voyages to the obstinate rocks:

I have known in my life no comparable theatrical experience to the dancing of Natalia Makarova; it is a world of its own, magically lit by music which is its own light, where there is a great calm, the quiet ordering of vast harmonies, in one body the movement of eternal spheres. No words can contain it, this miracle of art which is her's alone, where the dance and the dancer are one.

132

# *Epilogue*

As ONE of the finest and most experienced dancers of the Royal Ballet said to me while I was writing this book, 'Every dancer who takes the stage appears there naked'. To dance in truth and with sincerity is to expose the deepest secrets of one's nature; it is the most direct of all communications between human beings.

The beauty of Natalia Makarova's character, so vital, generous and without any sort of pettiness or spite, at once vulnerable and child-like, easily wounded yet truly forgiving, is contained—the the whole of it—in her dancing. I do not need gossip or startling revelations to describe the person she is; I need only her dancing on the stage when she speaks to us from the secrecy of her own heart.

Now at last this is fully recognised by the public, who were in some ways so reluctant to accept her after she left the Kirov Ballet to dance in the West. The huge roar of applause that greeted her first performance with Mikhail Baryshnikov in *Le Sacre du Printemps* at the London Coliseum last year seemed to me to confirm all my beliefs about her that I had held for so long. My mind went back to that *Giselle* of sixteen years ago, to the dancer whose genius I had glimpsed then and whose progress I had charted with such passionate concern.

There was no longer any case to argue, as I had argued it so many times before. I was like a person who had talked all night about the coming brilliance of the dawn, and now what I had said was obvious in the brightness of high noon. I considered, rather sadly, as I left the theatre that I can now leave her greatness for others to explore. For me the adventure was over; about Natalia Makarova I had said my last word. In one respect, however, I have failed, since the mystery of her genius I must leave unsolved, even though it reaches us in truth and total sincerity in the visionary landscape of her art.

# Index of Ballets

135

# INDEX OF BALLETS

# Index of Names

# INDEX OF NAMES

# INDEX OF NAMES